"UNDER THE TOUGH OLD STARS"
Ecopedagogical Essays

"UNDER THE TOUGH OLD STARS"

Ecopedagogical Essays

David W. Jardine
University of Calgary

A Solomon Press Book

The Foundation for Educational Renewal, Inc.

"UNDER THE TOUGH OLD STARS" Ecopedagogical Essays
by David W. Jardine

The Foundation for Educational Renewal, Inc.
P.O. Box 328
Brandon, VT 05733
phone: 800-639-4122
http://www.PathsOfLearning.net

Some of these essays originally appeared in other publications. We give thanks and acknowledgement: "'Under the Tough Old Stars'" in Canadian Journal of Environmental Education (1, spring, 1996, pp. 48-55);"'Returning Home with Empty Hands'" in Reflections on Pedagogy and Method, volume I, edited by R. Evans and M. Van Manen (Calgary: Faculty of Education, University of Calgary, pp. 143-157); "The Surroundings" in The Journal of Curriculum Theorizing (13, 3, pp. 18-31); "'Littered with Literacy'" in Journal of Curriculum Studies (26,5, pp. 509-524); "The Stubborn Particulars of Grace'" in Experience and the Curriculum: Principles and Programs, edited by B. Horwood (Dubuque, IA: Kendall/Hunt Publishing Company, pp. 261-275); "Ecopedagogical Reflectsion" in Alberta Science Education Journal (27,1, pp. 50-56); "Reflections on Education, Hermeneutics, and Ambiguity" in Understanding Curriculum as Phenomenological and Deconstructed Text, edited by W. Pinar and W. Reynolds (New York, NY: Teacher's College Press, pp. 116-130); "Birding Lessons and the Teachings of Cicadas" in Canadian Journal of Environmental Education (3, pp. 92-99); "Chapter 32 from 'Speaking with a Boneless Tongue'" in Speaking with a Boneless Tongue, by D. Jardine (Bragg Creek: Makyo*Press, ch. 32); "Piaget's Clay and Descartes' Wax" in Educational Theory (38, 3, pp. 287-298); "Unable to Return to the Gods that Made Them" in Unfolding Bodymind: Exploring Possibility Through Education, edited by B. Hocking, W. Linds, and J. Haskell (Brandon, VT: The Foundation for Educational Renewal); "All Beings Are Your Ancestors" in The Trumpeter: A Journal of Ecosophy (14, 3, pp. 122-123).

This book was designed by Sidney Solomon
and typeset by Eve Brant in Bodoni and Eras fonts

First printing September, 2000   ISBN: 1-885580-06-1

Contents

DEDICATION

This collection is dedicated to David G. Smith, a man who has saved my life more than once; to Patricia Clifford and Sharon Friesen, two teachers who helped me understand not only what the real work might be, but who first showed me that it can actually happen in real and ordinary schools; and especially my dear, sweet wife Gail, a great teacher and patient love; and my son Eric, in his own way a teacher, crouched, on the cover, on a rock in the Elbow River which appears so often in these pages.

Finally, this collection is dedicated to all those teachers and children who are suffering in the confines of schools. Hopefully they can find some breath here and can read these essays back to me in ways I cannot do alone.

Preface

by
DAVID GEOFFREY SMITH

International Forum
on Education and Society,
Department of Secondary
Education, University of Alberta

TOUGH OLD STARS. Every once in a while, even tough old stars converge in a way such that a child is born who brings light to the world. So most ancient mythologies say, and perhaps this is apposite with respect to David Jardine. Of course "light," as in bringing light to the world, means many things. The *Oxford English Dictionary* (ninth edition) groups the meanings into two, one having to do with illumination, the other with issues of weight, that is, how things are borne by the earth. In the first group, number one seems appropriate: "The natural agent...that stimulates sight, and makes things visible." Some others are useful too: "A flame or spark serving to ignite;" "Vivacity, enthusiasm, or inspiration visible in a person's face, esp. in the eyes;" even "Set burning or begin to burn." In the second group, number eight is perfect: "Nimble, quick moving."

The very multiplicity of these meanings is itself relevant, given the profoundly hermeneutical quality of David Jardine's work. By hermeneutical, I mean the ability to see life as infinitely interpretable, which is not to swoon into dogmatic relativism, as in some postmodern writing. Instead it means to see life as an open book, which can be, indeed must be, constantly read and re-read as the essential condition of our freedom, humanly speaking. Without the vigilant exercise of hermeneutic imagination, received traditions of knowledge, even wisdom, become brutish and inert.

This, I believe, is the essential contribution of David Jardine's scholarship—his amazing ability to read life inside out, upside down, front and back. And this profound hermeneutical sensibility in David's case is neither random nor fickle nor supercilious. Instead it arises out of a deep understanding and appreciation of both Eastern and Western intellectual traditions, applied to some of the most pressing issues of our time, especially concerning pedagogy and the environment, and how, as a Western tradition in particular, we have come to a condition of such violence with respect to both.

David's undergraduate work was in the area of religious studies, especially Asian religion. His graduate work was, first, in formal philosophy with a Master's thesis investigating Edmund Husserl's transcendental phenomenology. His doctoral dissertation explored Jean Piaget's genetic epistemology of childhood. Reading this book, one can see how this intellectual journeying was foundational for the work taken up with such passion here. But one can conjecture too that this was not a peaceful, smooth evolution. Instead, one can sense in these essays moments of deep and difficult turning, true changes in consciousness as new understandings were brought to bear on old problems, such that the old problems are now seen more clearly as complicit in the construction of contemporary difficulties.

There is one paper in this collection that I believe is

absolutely pivotal for understanding the general orientation of David's work—"Piaget's Clay and Descartes' Wax."
The earliest essay in the book (1988), it is also a work that,
because of its sheer brilliance, and the importance of its
topic, should be read and re-read by every graduate student in every university department of every discipline.
Why such an assessment? Because in that essay David
undertakes a painstaking and detailed philosophical labor
of love to understand how contemporary child study, and
hence our common-sense pedagogical understandings of
child development, are linked through the work of Piaget
to the particular tyranny of intellectual and eventual cultural self enclosure that is at the heart of the Western tradition. I cannot recapitulate the arguments in this space,
except to trace the lineage as David does, through Descartes
to the epistemological revolution of Immanuel Kant, and
the particular trajectory of theorizing that lead Kant to claim
that "reason cannot come upon that which is other than its
own determination."

Here we have a conceptual key for unpacking two fundamental assumptions still at play in the self-understanding of the West: a) that it is the application of Reason that
enables an understanding of the world because b) it is in
the nature of the world that it is reasonable. The main im-
plication of this position is that the social and cultural Other
who arrives as a stranger (the difficult child, the ethnic,
linguistic, tribal Other, etc.) is immediately confronted with
a civilizational edifice that cannot, indeed will not, open
itself to the Other as an equal partner on any shared journey the outcome of which old Reason cannot imagine in
advance. Such is the conceptual architecture of hegemony,
and it has widespread consequences. The most prominent
example is the global dominance of Western science as a

presumed final arbiter of anything worth knowing. In the age of globalization, it is Western economic theory (especially its American radical free-market version) taken as science that may be the most dangerous conceit yet to be challenged. In the pedagogical realm, the reduction of the Child to an object of rational investigation and manipulation has lead teaching into a form of hell, as children stubbornly refuse to conform to the rational schemas of human development we have earnestly set for them, and teachers and students end up facing each other helplessly across a great divide, as two solitudes without the conceptual means for breaching the source of their mutual pain. Ecologically, the "real" world must be only the one we construct rationally and the rest can be sentimentalized inchoately as "just like us," waiting for us, to be discovered by us and hence given legitimacy. Basically it reduces the whole of life to a form of tourism over which our self-constructed sense of Reason presides.

So that is the first pivot I see in David's work—a deep excavation of his own received tradition, with a coming up for air, wondering how to proceed now, knowing that the tradition is exhausted. The next turn is to the alienated Other, that is, to everything that has been excluded by the Enlightenment conceit. Like all truly creative advances however, this is based not on an adolescent rejection of the father, but on a taking up of the father's witnessed stumbling efforts to transcend his own difficulties. In the Western tradition, phenomenology and hermeneutics historically played this role, largely through Husserl's theory of intentionality, and its realization of the intersubjective nature of human understanding. I don't think about the world from a condition of pure ego; instead the world is already in me as I think about it, and my thinking is constantly changing as

I meet the world and it affects me. No more can Reason be taken as a finished condition and established as a presidium over human affairs. My meetings with Others affects what I think is reasonable. Deeper, more mature living can only be achieved, therefore, through genuine openness to what comes to meet me as new, as a stranger. And strangers too have their own ways of making sense of me, so that if there is to be truth between us, we must sit down as friends, and work it out. This is the real work, the tough work, and it is ongoing, and never finished, which explains its vivifying quality, its capacity for constant rejuvenation. Hermes was a young god, always.

In David Jardine's oeuvre, the turn to the Other, to openness and rejuvenation, finds its focus in two domains, ecology and pedagogy. This is not accidental, although maybe partly serendipitous. I first met David in 1986 at the inaugural meeting of the Canadian Society for Hermeneutics and Postmodern Thought, held in Winnipeg, Manitoba. After giving his paper (on Piaget), he made his way to a job interview at the University of Calgary. It was for a position in early childhood education, and the interview was successful. Within six months of arriving in Calgary, he had bought a twenty-acre parcel of land in the foothills of the Rocky Mountains, and has lived there ever since. Pedagogy (how culture gets mediated in the lives of the young, for good or ill) and ecology (how we mediate our relations with the natural world, for good or ill) have been his defining passions for fifteen years now. His reflections on both must be seen as inseparable. Meditating on the Other of magpies, spruce trees, bears, coyotes, and cougars brings one to a realization of the interlocutionary possibilities of human/wild discourse, and there are profound implications for pedagogy.

One of the most telling examples still haunts me, months after reading the manuscript of this book. Walking one day in the woods, observing everything peacefully, with interest, David suddenly realized that though he had been looking at things all during the walk, for the entire duration too he had been "spotted" by every living thing. Really, he had been seen, before he saw. Squirrels, ants, birds, foxes—all of these had registered his coming, through various warning systems and calls, long before he set his own eyes upon them. The world is always, already there long before we say and do anything about it. A student is watching and measuring the teacher weeks before the first teacher-given test and progress evaluation report. A child's essential response to the world is already soul-coded before parental intervention strategies begin, so that effective parenting always involves working with the young, never simply "educating" them, and our own rejuvenation depends on how well we can listen to and hear what they are trying to teach us.

One last thing, related to this, maybe two. Several years ago at a conference I was speaking with a graduate student who earlier had been speaking with David. Quite spontaneously, she offered, "He's such an amazing listener!" Indeed. How could a person write the kind of brilliant, insightful essays contained in this book? Only someone who has listened deeply to the world, someone who has given careful witness, and who now bears witness to the real work that must be done if we are to truly care about our living could write this book. We are all made better by having such a one among us, a true bearer of light, and one who bears the light in the way light should be borne—lightly.

That is the one quality of David's that a text such as this may not be able to reflect adequately. To meet David personally means to encounter one the most screamingly funny men one is ever likely to meet. His wit is the perfect counterpoint, the inevitable outcome perhaps, of his hermeneutic seriousness. To hold them together as he does is something wonderful to behold. I consider it a deep honor to call him a friend.

LEARNING TO WORK
UNDER THE TOUGH
OLD STARS

A GREAT DEAL of my day-to-day work as a university professor consists of practicum supervision in local elementary schools and teaching courses connected to elementary school curricula. One of the frustrations of such work is having to face how schoolrooms are, for the most part, understood to be the most ordinary and commonplace of places, and how, in fact, they are most odd. It seems, on the face of it, that the work that ensues in such places is straightforwardly mundane. But these places our children are required to inhabit, day after day, week after week, year after year are, in fact, neither straightforward nor especially mundane. They are often quite other-worldly.

However, as my dear friend David G. Smith said to me once, the good news and the bad news are often hand –in hand.

On the one hand, schools are premised on an often unvoiced, pernicious, ecologically disastrous metaphysical tenet. What is understood to be "basic" to any of the living disciplines with which schools have been entrusted are its smallest, most easily assessable and deliverable bits and pieces. What rarely seems to occur under this strange

1

auspice is that such fragmentation, such analytic dissasemblage of language and mathematics and art and the arts of science is, in fact, a highly arcane, highly theoretical accomplishment. In a terrible turn of events, the *results* of this accomplishment (an accomplishment *to which our children are not party*) are portioned out to the youngest of our children because these isolated bits and pieces are understood to be "more basic" that the living disciplines from which they have been culled.

We *live* with our children in the living inheritance of these disciplines—an inheritance which is, of course, both shared and contested, admired and despised, and as globally unavoidable as it is culturally rooted. However, once these disciplines become schooled, they are no longer places we might inhabit, places where we might work out our relations to these difficulties, these telling, mixed, and multiple ancestries and bloodlines. They become, rather, inert objects, doled out in monitored relations of exchange. And we forget. The youngest child is handed a mathematics work sheet to "do" as if it is the most ordinary thing in the world, as if it actually somehow *exists* out of relation to all things, out of relation to the living, human hands that have handed mathematics to us as something we were supposed to take care of, supposed to cultivate, renew, reform, transform. We forget that we must decide what, perhaps even *whether*, we were going to tell our children of its existence and of the loving work it will require of them if it is to remain hale and healthy and generous and true.

Right in the midst of this strange turn of events, in comes "environmental education." It is no surprise that it, too, often falls prey to this very same metaphysical tenet. It has become, in many schools, one more damn thing that needs the weary and already scattered and overburdened attention of teachers and children. Paradoxically, the earth, as the topic of "environmental education," becomes one topic among others. To the extent that this occurs, something is terribly wrong, not because this topic should be pre-eminent (as is often the understandably heated urging of environmentalists), but because *there must be some sense in which there is no other topic*, some sense in which *all* the living disciplines in our care are earthly inheritances in need of precisely the same mindfulness and imagination and tough work. If we imagine that *there is* another topic than our living on earth, the ecological disaster has *already occurred*, no matter how loud the voice of environmentalism then becomes, and no matter how vital the work it then pursues.

This is one of the reasons for the neologism "ecopedagogy." It is an attempt to find ways in which ecologically rich images of ancestry, sustainability, interrelatedness, interdependency, kinship, and topography can help revitalize our understanding of *all* of the living disciplines in our care. With the essays in this collection I attempt to identify the logic of fragmentation that underwrites contemporary schooling, and the ecologically disastrous equation of what is "basic" with what is isolated and out of relation. But here is where the bad news turns out to be the good news. Right in the midst of the most ordinary of seemingly isolated school events lies the possibility of a sort of "seeing through." It is useless, I have found, to try to argue against the metaphysical tenet of fragmentation and isolation with another metaphysical tenet of wholeness and relatedness. It is useless because it is precisely proceeding metaphysically that is the problem. An ecologically mindful sense of relatedness, as a truly imaginable and practicable phenomenon in our schools, always occurs *here* and *here*. It is never a matter, for example, of turning our backs on this horrible little mathematics work sheet. That is too easy and simply abandons it and abandons those abandoned to such trivializations. We must summon the courage to stare it down, open it up to the voices hiding not elsewhere, but *within* it. We must begin the difficult work of breaking open the seemingly hard, unforgiving surface of this most ordinary of things and seeing how right here, in the midst of this very mundaneity, "the gods themselves are present."

This has become a frequent topic of conversation in many of my classes. Faced with the dulling and leveling character of school practices, many student-teachers want to do grander things. They look in the language arts curriculum guides, for example, and berate the fact that they have to teach "commas" because they remember all too well how deadly such a prospect can be for all concerned. They want, instead, to let children be creative and let them write their own stories, because they deeply and desperately want to help children out from under the dead weight that they themselves suffered in their own schooling. The problem is that this has the potential of simply replacing one betrayal with another. Worse yet, it sets up the conditions under which a "conservative" backlash comes roaring it, full of fundamentalist confidence and anger, touting zero-tolerance and announcing a version of "back to the basics" that keeps in place all the old logics. And this, in turn, sets up the conditions under which a "liberal" backlash comes roaring in speaking about self-esteem and ebullience. And this, in turn, turns again.

The tough work is avoiding simply doing the inverse of what we despise, because, as an inverse, we remain tethered to and dependent upon that which we despise. We must step away from these alternatives we have been handed and all the old battles that they inevitiably require. These battles are *themselves* ecological disasters, because they portend either a traditional world that requires no renewal, or a world of newness that requires nothing old. This is why I've pursued the idea of ecopedagogy, as an attempt to "step away" from what has become an exhausting and, I believe, exhausted debate in education.

Ecopedagogically, the question is this: How can we release ourselves to experience the wondrous, generative, fecund, powerful, living, irreplaceable character of something so seemingly commonplace as commas? How is it that we have forgotten that these seemingly most ordinary and mundane of things live in the midst of our language, that they trace the contours of our breathing and pausing like nothing else, that they have a living place in this living place that is speaking and writing, and, to be deeply understood, to be deeply experienced, they must not be bypassed in favor of some woozy sense of wholeness, but experienced as precisely a way in to the living wholeness of language, written or spoken?

Differently put, how can we help ourselves and our children remember that this world of ours—for example, the living world of language, the living world of mathematics—is deeply and pleasurably *interpretable*? How can we help ourselves and our children remember that such interpretability is not an accidental add-on to some intransigent given, but is necessary to a *living* discipline? How can we learn to work under these tough old stars and not betray the lovely, toiling, agonizing character of such work?

I'd love to start this next paragraph with "Well, first of all..." but in education we've already had enough quick, attractively packaged, sure-fired, soon-outdated versions of *that* to last a lifetime. All of us in education have seen too many promises broken and we are coming to learn a hard lesson from the insights of ecological mindfulness. A consequence of the metaphysical logic of fragmentation is precisely hurriedness, and there are few places as hurried as schools. However, if we can imagine mathematics and language and science and art and social studies as living topographies, living places full of spooks and spirits and lives and voices, we find that learning to live well in such living places, learning to take good care of them, learning their ways, takes time—often a long time—often longer than the life we've each been allotted. It often requires years of suffering, trying again, listening anew, speaking and thinking and changing your mind, meticulous, sometimes boring memorization and imitation of those who have come before us, trial, error, trial again, breakthrough and breakdown and resolve.

This is something we have always known about those things worthy of our attention. It take time, patience, and a certain toughness to settle into a place and learn its lessons and learn what our real work might be, learning not simply the work we feel like doing, but the work that the place requires of us. The real work of learning to live under these tough old stars thus has to do with character, with standing and living in the presence of these living disciplines and *living with the consequences*, becoming someone who carries the marks of having sojourned here, of having not taken the cheap way out, despite the tremendous cultural drags towards cheapness, triviality, and disposability that haunt us all at nearly every turn.

It is not unlike Wendell Berry suggested about the farmer who plants a row of trees as a testament to the willingness and desire and decision to *stay put* and do what needs to be done, even if the farmer may not live to witness the fullness of the trees' growing.

The essays in this collection range over twelve years and have been collected from various sources—some from journals and book chapters, some from desk drawer bottoms or other odd hiding places. They represent a desire to stay put. But there is more than this. I've found that it has been *possible* to stay put here in this alluring ecopedagogical terrain that I've happened upon. This discourse has allowed me to learn, slowly and painfully, to love the mundane eventfulness of schooling as a place that is both frustrating and pleasurable, but still decidedly both worthy of and in need of interpretation. Also, when student teachers and practicing teachers fall prey to the old logics of fragmentation, I'm learning to no longer hate them for their complicity, but to love them for bearing this burden on behalf of us all. Because unless they bear it and live it out, it will remain hidden and still at work.

One thing you will find as you wander through these essays is that many voices repeat, many passages are cited in different contexts and from different angles. I have decided to leave such repetitions in place because hopefully they can work as reminders. But, more than this, when the shared and contested ancestries we carry with us are called to account, they are always called to account *in the face of* the stubborn particularity of events that need their witness. Therefore, what is, on the face of it, a repeated passage is hopefully also, something that comes to mean something new because of the newness of the event which has demanded something of it *here*, in *this* place, under these tough old stars. Thus, as another lesson of ecological mindfulness, even those long, convoluted, and sometimes seemingly irrelevant philosophical traditions that underwrite our pedagogical and ecological troubles, face the sometimes painful, sometimes uproariously joyous possibility of renewal and recovery from their schooled deadliness.

So begins the work under these tough old stars.

CHAPTER One

"UNDER THE TOUGH OLD STARS"

Meditations on Pedagogical
Hyperactivity and the Mood
of Environmental Education

"under the tough old stars—
To the real work, to
"What is to be done."
(Gary Snyder, from I Went Into the Maverick Bar)

I

T HE TERM "ENVIRONMENTAL EDUCATION" can give us pause to consider how ecological awareness, ecological attunement, might be more than simply a particular topic among others in the classroom. It might help us glimpse how it is that *education itself*, in its attention to all the disciplines that make up schooling, can be conceived as deeply ecological in character and mood.

Ecology can provide us with images that help us re-conceive the traditions and disciplines of education as themselves deeply ecological communities of relations, full of long, convoluted histories, full of life and lives, traditions and wisdoms that require our "continuity of attention and devotion" (Berry, 1986, p. 34) if they are to remain generous, sustainable and true, if they are to remain *liv-*

9

able. For example, mathematics can become conceived as
a rich, imaginative place, full of topographies and histories and tales to tell, full of relations of kin and kind, full of
deep patterns and powers. Mathematics might become conceived as itself a deeply interconnected, earthly phenomenon, linked to patterns of breath and bone, bearing
kinships to patterns of language and song, linked, too, to
symmetries etched in stone, to the spiral doings of leaves,
and to the sun downarching towards *sol stasis* and returning.

Ecology can also provide images of what it would mean
to talk of the classroom as a real, living community, full of
traces of the old and the young, the new and the established, and the often difficult conversations between them.
Classrooms, too, can become full of a commitment to working out and working through those wisdoms and disciplines
and traditions and tales, shared and contested, that have
been handed down to us all. It can be a place full, in a
deeply ecological sense, of "real work" (Snyder, 1980;
Clifford & Friesen, 1993).

II

. . .the connections, the dependencies, remain. To
damage the earth is to damage your children. (Wendell
Berry, from The Unsettling of America)

Ecological awareness always and already involves the
presence of our children. Ecology thus always already involves images of pedagogy and the teaching and learning
of the tales that need to be told for all of us to live well. As
with pedagogy, ecology is always already intergenerational
(Friesen, Clifford & Jardine, 1998).

In this way, we can conceive of disciplines such as poetry, or negative and positive integers, or the histories of this land, as large, generous places, full of relations in which we might learn to live well, adding our work to these places, our memories and voices, our arguments and alternatives and differences. We can now ask of education itself that it help to develop:

> . . .the sense of "nativeness," of belonging to the place. Some people are beginning to try to understand where they are, and what it would mean to live carefully and wisely, delicately in a place, in such a way that you can live there adequately and comfortably. Also, your children and grandchildren and generations a thousand years in the future will still be able to live there. That's thinking as though you were a native. Thinking in terms of the whole fabric of living and life. (Snyder, 1980, p. 86)

Understood in this earthy, intergenerational way, education (and not just "environmental education" as a sub-branch, most often, of science education) has the opportunity, perhaps the obligation, to slow down the pace of attention, to broaden out its own work into the long-standing patterns and places we inhabit and which inhabit us.

It has the opportunity, perhaps the obligation, to take on a mood not unlike ecological mindfulness.

III

> Manic pace is cultivated as a virtue in elementary schools. Teachers getting kids to run from place to place, activity to activity. All noise and no sounds. Quiet is undervalued as only the quiet of straight rows—made

to be quiet by somebody, not being quiet. (Patricia
Clifford, a teacher at Ernest Morrow Junior High School)

It is fascinating to consider how, in these ecologically
desperate days, just as ecology is heralding the need for a
continuity of attention and devotion, our schools are, in so
many cases, full of attention deficits (itself a wonderfully
co-opted marketing term along with its dark twin, "paying
attention"). This is coupled with a sort of hyperactivity that
precludes the slowing of pace and the broadening of attention to relations and interdependencies that love and devotion to a place require of us.

This all-too-apt image—"getting kids to run from place
to place, activity to activity"—is clearly not a phenomenon that appears simply in elementary schools. Rather, it
is endemic to what is now widely described as post-modern
culture in North America: an onslaught of frenetic, discon-
nected, fragmented images and free-floating meanings, a
twirling free play of signs and signifiers and surfaces, none
of which requires or deserves care or attention, none of
which has a strong or vital link to any other fragment. In
this flickering place, nothing *pertains* and therefore, of
course, we can do whatever we desire. We make all the
patterns or connections and they can, at our beck and call,
always be undone and redone as we like. Loosed, here, is
an image of the human subject as isolated from any deep
obligation or complicity or relation to anything. Loosed here,
too, is the portend of ecological disaster.

Think, for example of television channel surfing, or,
more recently, "surfing the net."

If the surface is all there is, then surfing is all that is
required.

I can always, as one Grade Seven student put it,

"switch" if things get demanding or bog down or become no longer amusing or stimulating.

And, of course, as with surfing, if one loses momentum, if one hesitates for a moment, you're sunk.

Consider this horrible image:

> The subject of postmodernity is best understood as the ideal-type channel-hopping MTV viewer who flips through different images at such speed that she/he is unable to chain the signifiers together into a meaningful narrative, he/she merely enjoys the multiphrenic intensities and sensations of the surface of the images. (Usher & Edwards, 1994, p. 11)

And, in light of such a subject, the corpus of the world and the traditions we are living out become "part of the emporium of styles to be promiscuously dipped into. It becomes yet another experience to be sampled—neither intrinsically better or worse" (pp. 11-12).

In this milieu, meaning and significance and connection get reduced to glinting surface stimulation. And since stimulation is inherently always momentary, new stimulation is always needed—new "activities" are always underway. And so we have a common feature of many schools— a relentless rush from activity to activity, all in the name of "keeping the children's interest."

Once this occurs, it is little wonder that panic sets in. And it is little wonder that Wendell Berry (1986) suggests that it is precisely this sort of unsettled panic that makes us excellent consumers of ever more and more activities.

Just as ecology has been suggesting, we find ourselves in schools helplessly feeding the voracious activity beast, finding ourselves sometimes taken by the exhilarating rush of it all, and finding ourselves unwittingly equating the ends of education with being able, in deft post-modern fashion, to manipulate surfaces to one's own ends and to live consumptively.

IV

Perhaps the "ADD kids" in our classrooms can be understood to be like canaries in a mine shaft—warnings, portents, heralds, like the monstrous, transgressive child often is (Jardine, 1994; Clifford & Friesen, 1995; Clifford, Friesen & Jardine, 1995), that airs have thinned and sustaining relations have been broken and need healing. Perhaps they are signs that education needs to become a form of ecological healing (Clifford & Friesen, 1994)—mending "all my relations."

A mending done through the recovery, through our teaching, of the generous wisdoms and patterns of the world.

This is the juncture where education can become environmental in a deep sense. It can be the place where we might slow the attention and broaden our relations to the earth.

Consider, for example, the deep pleasures to be had in the mathematical symmetries and geometric curves of just this yellow leaf corkscrewing down from a late fall Cottonwood, and how it heralds the arc of seasons and the movements of planets and suns, and the bodily desires for shelter, and how many have stood here like this, stock still, trying to read the deep patterns and dignities and eloquences of this place:

> I think probably the rhythm I'm drawing on most now is the whole of the landscape of the Sierra Nevada, to

feel it all moving underneath. There is the periodicity of ridge, gorge, ridge, gorge, ridge, gorge at the spur ridge and the tributary gorges that make an interlacing network of, oh, 115-million-year-old geological formation rhythms. I'm trying to feel through that more than anything else right now. All the way down to some Tertiary gravels which contain a lot of gold from the Pliocene. Geological rhythms. I don't know how well you can to do that in poetry. Well, like this for example. Have you ever tried singing a range of mountains? (Snyder, 1980, p. 4)

Consider this reminder that the desire to utter this place up into the eloquences of language and rhyme is itself ecological work, the work of a place, and the work of the breath:

The rhythm of a song or a poem rises, no doubt, in reference to the pulse and breath of the poet. But that is too specialized an accounting; it rises also in reference to daily and seasonal—and surely even longer— rhythms in the life of the poet and in the life that surrounds him. The rhythm of a poem resonates with these larger rhythms that surround it; it fills its environment with sympathetic vibrations. Rhyme, which is a function of rhythm, may suggest this sort of resonance; it marks the coincidences of smaller structures with larger ones, as when the day, the month, and the year all end at the same moment. Song, then, is a force opposed to speciality and to isolation. It is the testimony of the singer's inescapable relation to the earth, to the human community, and also to tradition. (Berry, 1983, p. 17)

Consider that perhaps our rhyming utterance of this leaf-fall "leads one to hear an ancient cosmology"

(Meschonnic, 1988, p. 93) that is folded into language and breath itself.

. . .so that just this leaf opens countless tales, each one of which is about all the others, each one of which holds and deepens and quiets and places all the others.

. . .the pace of attention slows and broadens and becomes more stable, less frantic. We don't need to speed ahead, to keep up, to crowd and cram the classroom with activity after activity. We can slow and settle and return.

. . .so that just this leaf becomes the portal or opening in to a Great Council of All Beings gathering in interweaving relations, and suddenly it sits still, settled, and the whole of things starts to corkscrew around its stillness.

And then, just in time, Coyote shows up, ready to tweak the nose of such ecological self-seriousness, watching the selfsame:

> Beautiful little gold colored Cottonwood leaves floating down to the ground, and they go this. . .this. . .this. . . this. . .this, this this this, and he just watches those for the longest time. Then he goes up and he asks those leaves "Now how do you do that? That's so pretty the way you come down." And they say, "Well there's nothing to it, you just get up in a tree, and then you fall off." So he climbs up the Cottonwood tree and launches himself off, but he doesn't go all pretty like that, he just goes bonk and kills himself." (Snyder, 1977, pp. 70-1)

But, as we know, "Coyote never dies, he gets killed plenty of times, and then he goes right on travelling" (p. 71), teaching a little lesson on the way, that these patterns of leaves falling are their own, and remember where you are and who you are, and it's getting cold, and enough writing, and it's time to get the wind kicked up to hot breath walking again.

V

Just as with much of our lives, many classrooms are full of cheap, trivial, laminate-thin hyperstimulants meant to titillate, amuse, or seduce us into wanting more. Just as with so many of us, many schools are full of teachers ravaged by the skittering activity that has become their daily work.

Education, environmentally understood, requires that we refuse to participate in this ecological disaster. It requires that we find work to do, for ourselves and our children, that bears some dignity and earthly discipline—good stories, large fields of thought, "big ideas" (Clifford & Friesen, 1993) that need children to re-think them, that are *that* generous and true.

As always with ecological work, the work begins at home. There is no one left over here to demonize. It is always first *my own* attention and devotion to the world and its ways that is at issue, my own ability and willingness to pursue experiences that deepen as they proceed, and to refuse, when I can, as I can, experience-as-(hyper)activity, experience-as-distraction.

The problem, however, is that healing the flittering of attention that underwrites much of our lives cannot be had quickly or painlessly or finally. Remaining alert, remaining open to new experiences, is always a task to be taken up again, from here, with these children, this year, with these wisdoms of the world.

We cannot do to children what we have not already done to ourselves (Clifford & Friesen, 1994). We cannot deepen their wisdom of and attention to the earth and its ways until we have first taken on the work of this wisdom and attention ourselves.

CHAPTER Two

"RETURNING HOME
WITH EMPTY HANDS"

I

It is impossible to divorce the question of what we do from the question of where we are—or, rather, where we think we are. That no sane creature befouls its own nest is accepted as generally true. What we conceive to be our nest, where we think it is, are therefore questions of the greatest importance. (Berry, 1986, p. 51)

DURING THE RECENT twentieth anniversary celebrations of the first moon landing, one of the former Apollo astronauts was asked how he would sum up what the Apollo program was all about. He replied, "It's about leaving."

It is interesting to speculate as to whether there is any interconnection between the lack of success in generating any great excitement about "further, deeper penetration into the solar system" and "getting it [the program] up again" (and a great deal of other unintentionally but still rather blatantly phallocentric talk), and the recent flourishing of ecological awareness. For ecological awareness is not about leaving, but about responsibly staying put here on earth. It has to do with the logos of our home, our dwelling, and with how we can come to be at home here in a way that does not overstep the real possibilities of dwelling responsibly, sanely, in a way that does not befoul the very "nest" that houses us. Ecology is therefore about returning our attention to home. It is about tending anew to where we dwell, to our nest, to the delicate and difficult reliances and debts that intertwine our fleshy lives with the fleshy life of the earth; it is this moist texture that bestows our lives and makes them possible. Becoming attentive to this original bestowal, this "original blessing" (Fox, 1983) requires more than "understanding" and "knowing" as they have come to be. Our issuing up out of the earth is not a set of objective relations that we can place in front of us for our perusal. Understanding such issuance requires cultivating "the continuity of attention and devotion without which the human life of the earth is impossible. The care of the earth is our most ancient and most worthy and, after all, our most pleasing responsibility. To cherish what remains of it, and to foster its renewal, is our only legitimate hope." (Berry, 1986, p. 14)

Attention, devotion, care, worthiness, cherishing, fostering, renewal, hope: these are not just any words. They echo a deep sense of place, of remaining, of dwelling, of settling. These words bring with them a sense of memory and continuity and regeneration, a mindfulness of what is needed for life to go on, and a passing of such mindfulness to the young. Children are already present in these words. "Leaving" once described our fanciful hopes for the future. It is now becoming one of the traumatic and painful features of ecological insight—we cannot just leave, for the exhaust(ion) left in the wake of such leaving inevitably returns, and, just as inevitably, it always returns precisely here. Even if the ecological consequences of our actions do not return to this specific place, we return here slightly more insane, slightly more "out of place," "out of touch" with where we really are. We carry this consequence in our hearts along with the displaced and displacing belief that we live somewhere other than on the whole of the earth, needing to believe, to protect our sanity, that we have left those consequences "someplace else."

If home is abandoned altogether—if we all get caught up in "leaving"—our care for and devotion to the conditions, sources, and intimate dependencies of renewal and generativity are also abandoned; and with these is abandoned our only legitimate hope (van Manen, 1983). And if we abandon our care for and devotion to the conditions of renewal and generativity, we abandon our care for and devotion to our children.

Ecopedagogical reflection thus involves drawing together our concern, as educators, for the presence of new life in our midst (Smith, 1988) (and for bringing forth this new life into the world, our world—educare) and "our most pleasing responsibility," caring for the earth. Such reflection simply asks: In what ways do questions of pedagogy interweave with questions of the continued existence of an earth in the embrace of which pedagogy is possible? Ecology and pedagogy interweave to the extent that separating them or separating our responsibilities for them can be accomplished only at a tragic cost. "No matter the distinctions we draw, the connections, the dependencies, remain. To damage the earth is to damage our children." (Berry, 1986, p. 57) Perhaps we will see that pedagogy, too, is "our most pleasing responsibility." It, too, requires the very same

love, care, and generosity of spirit that ecological awareness does. Ecology is silently and inevitably interwoven
with pedagogy. In the face of this interweaving, we cannot
just "leave."

II

Loving and savoring the articulate beauty of mathematics is interlaced with the ability to love and savor the actual conditions under which the doing of mathematics is
possible. The indigenous articulations and beautiful inner
workings and intimate interrelationships of mathematics
must be re-thought anew as "human formations" (Husserl,
1970, p. 170) in the full, embodied, "fleshed-out" sense—
full of humus, earthly. This rethinking has two moments,
the first rather long and convoluted, the second frighten-
ingly straightforward.

First is needed articulation of "that anciently perceived
likeness between all creatures and the earth of which they
are made" (Berry, 1983, p. 76). For example, "symmetry,"
as detailed in the Grade Two curriculum guide, is not some
abstract and cerebral "concept," but is right before us as
we stretch out our arms and clap our hands in time, right
there in the pinwheel patterning of this orange we divide
with this child, again in the turns we take dividing these
pieces (there also, implicit in the unfairness of "unsym-
metrical" turns), again in the radiating needles of this pine
tree outside the window, again in the rhythm and rhyme of
language, in the change of days, of seasons, and in the
cycled repetition of inhaling and exhaling.

Loving and savoring the articulate beauty of mathematics entails being mindful of how mathematics rests in the

embrace of the earth and re-sings the resonances and relationships that issue up out of the earth. It entails realizing that mathematical "forms" are not identical with our operations (Piaget, 1952): we do not make these connections. They are findings, anciently perceived. We "come upon them," abstract from them in the name of clarity and distinctness, and then all too easily forget their earthly origin. In spite of this, however, and even for the professional mathematician, the cycled rhythms of breath persist as a deeper and moister "knowing" of mathematics than its professional articulations might allow, a knowing that someone (to use Jean Piaget's formulation) "at the logico-mathematical stage of cognitive development" shares with the very young child, more deeply, with all of life: a common knowing, a "kinship" that the idealizations of the "discipline" of mathematics often appear to disavow. More pointedly, it can appear that it is precisely this disavowal of kinship that mathematics must profess in order to attain its discipline. Many of my student teachers deeply believe that clapping your hands in time to a song is not "really" mathematics. "Real" mathematics requires occult symbols and chalk and dust and the mechanical repetition of the meaningless, done as some sort of terrible, inevitable penance for being only human in the face of this Divine Science.

Here is the grand reversal that Edmund Husserl enacted with his phenomenology: it is not either necessary or possible to draw all of life up into the idealizations of mathematics and logic. Rather, our earthly life already resonates with ambiguous, living mathematical forms of which the well-bound "discipline" of mathematics is the idealization (Jardine, 1990). Realizing the mathematical character of breath is not a making profane the sacred discipline of mathematics. It is tying its idealizations back (*religare*) to their generative analogical sources. It is a re-membrance of its deeply earthly character. Mathematics lives and is at home here. Even its idealizations are earthly dreams, dreamt by humans. Mathematics is not only deeply about the life of the earth. It is a feature of that earthly life, laced to the logos of that home. It is the resting of math-ematics in the embrace of this generative source that makes it a living discipline, one that can always be re-thought, one that can always seduce us anew with its "eloquent ges-tures" (Merleau-Ponty, 1972, p. 42).

Ludwig Wittgenstein named this analogical interlac-ing "family resemblances" or "kinships" (1968. p. 32). The idealizations of mathematics are not identical to its sen-sorimotor, kinaesthetic, embodied analogues, but these analogues are the "kin" of mathematical idealizations. The young child, stretching out her arms and saying in an ever louder voice "I have a millllllion stickers at home" is dwell-ing in kinships to the mathematical notion of numerical "quantity"—the stretch of arms, the increasing volume of voice and the "stretching" out of the word "million" dis-plays a rich and ambiguous understanding of such a "big" (so to speak) number. The idealized mathematical notion of "numerical quantity" belongs here in the midst of this diversity of instantiations. That is to say, the idealized math-ematical notion is not of an aloof paradigm that sits "above" these instances; neither does it sit at the end of a develop-mental sequence of these instances. It is one of the in-stances, belonging here, on earth, with these other instances which are its "kin," its "kind."

Ecopedagogical reflection thus concerns the belonging-together-in-diversity of the full range of human understanding. It is these anciently perceived likenesses or "family resemblances" that make children our kind (and them, with us, the kind of the earth). And it is this anciently perceived kinship that makes the most fundamental pedagogical (and ecological) response one of "kindness." It is these anciently perceived likenesses or family resemblances that make the earth our home, and therefore make the most fundamental ecological (and pedagogical) response also one of "kindness."

If these analogical links are not recovered, mathematics begins to appear to be capable of drawing up into itself and becoming identical with its idealized articulations (precisely the sort of hard, fossilized notion of science that Husserl critiqued). We can imagine ourselves breaking the threads of kinship and likeness that bind our lives to the life of the earth (such idealization is possible, as is the forgetfulness that goes along with it). Mathematics can appear to be no longer at home here (just like our sad inheritance of the Cartesian "I think" that orients the "subjection" we bring upon the earth). Once we can imagine the threads of kinship being severed, we then find that the pristine and articulate beauty of mathematics can henceforth take it upon itself to make demands upon the earth out of which it has arisen. The clarity and distinctness of Descartes' "I think" became the criterion of any re-connection to the earth that could make a claim to knowledge—that is, we are only connected to things again insofar as that connection is forged with the clarity and distinctness of self-presence. Once the original kinship and "at-homeness" on the earth has been lost, the achieved clarity of mathematics is turned back upon the earth as a weapon of domination. The earth becomes an inert thing to which mathematics owes nothing and which it can henceforth inseminate with its own forms. Mathematics, looking upon itself in its own image, imagines that it has not issued up out of the earth, that it has no kinship to this place, that it is not at home here. For it to feel at home here, it must violate what is here by giving order(s) of its own meticulous making.

Consequently, to dwell here is not to be mindful of this place and its delicate contours, but to make this place "mind." Mathematics owes only to itself, needing nothing but itself in order to exist. (This is a paraphrase of Descartes' notion of substance, taken from the Scholastic, and earlier, Aristotelian traditions.) Mathematics is at home only with itself and with that which it produces after its own image. It cannot tolerate infestations with anything other than that which it has itself formed. Mathematics and its brethren (formal logic and the meticulous methods of the sciences) thus become the home (office) from which order(s) is (are) issued. The moist and ambiguous contours of the earth and our delicate kinships with our home become violated, colonized with demands for unequivocal clarity and distinctness. Logico-mathematical operations become the right of passage (colon—home office is where the colonized must get a "pass") for the earth. The whole earth must pass through the sphincter of Reason because (it is believed) without the organizing activity of (adult, white, male, European) human intervention, the earth possess no indigenous "order" of its own.

In the face of this colonizing impulse, the earth becomes what the colonizer has always understood any Other (women, children, foreigners, different races, creeds, colors, smells) to be: dark, disorderly, unorganized, unruly, unmethodical, unreasonable, unreliable, untrustworthy, possessing no indigenous integrity at all, in desperate need of imposed order, needing to be "whipped into shape." (Consider the potential violence in naming children "our greatest natural resource.") In our self-enamorment, it becomes less and less possible to understand why the colonized refuse our gracious bestowals of law and order.

Here is the final(izing) pedagogical twist: the rejection of our gracious bestowals of order become incomprehensible betrayals, pointing to the fact that we have simply not been diligent enough. How could they do this to me after all I have done? I'll have to show them. (I can't help but hear the voice of Marc Lepine.) Violence. And, sad to say, violence with a pedagogic voice: We must teach these unruly "others" a lesson they'll never forget.

III

The second moment of ecopedagogical reflection is blunt and obvious. For pedagogy to be possible, there must be an earth which can sustain our lives. We cannot befoul the earth which grants us breath and then, with that very befouled breath, speak of the beauty of mathematics and of our eloquent pedagogical aspirations. And, bluntly put, we do this all the time, for we bear within our hearts a long and sad inheritance (sketched in the barest of detail above) of belief in the ascendancy of Reason, of humanity, of Europe, of being male, of the potency, irresistibility, and inherent morality of our own actions, our own dominion, of the immorality of not doing anything we can conceive of doing. And yet, the sting of ecological awareness faces this inheritance with the inevitability that

> It is not accumulated curricular knowledge that we deeply offer our children in educating them. It is not their epistemic excellence or their mastery of requisite

skills or their grade-point average, but literally their ability to live, their ability to be on an earth that will sustain their lives. A thorough grounding in mathematics is of little use if that knowledge is understood in such a way that there is no longer any real ground that is safe to walk. (Jardine, 1990, p. 112)

There is required, in ecopedagogical reflection, a sense of breaking through the Scholastic notion of "substance." It is difficult to comprehend, standing as we do in the shadow of Western and Christian philosophical traditions. A substance, in this tradition, is that which needs nothing but itself in order to exist. (Consider how much of a stake we have in this notion and how it underwrites images of American democracy and individuality.) The disorienting character of ecopedagogical insight lies precisely here: anything requires everything else in order to exist. Thereby, in attempting to understand, to know, to experience any one thing, all things are ushered forth in a nest of interdependencies with this one thing, interdependencies that cannot be severed without this thing's losing its integrity, its wholeness. This makes fully naming, fully understanding, fully experiencing, fully knowing this thing impossible. And this impossibility is not a matter of the nest of interdependencies being very large and complex. Rather, understanding and knowing and experiencing and naming are features of this nest of interdependencies.

IV

Ecological awareness begins and remains within a paradox regarding human life. We can do the impossible:

The unnoticeable law of the earth preserves the earth in the sufficiency of the emerging and perishing of all things in the allotted sphere of the possible which everything follows and yet nothing knows. The birch tree never oversteps its possibility. It is [human] will which drives the earth beyond the sphere of its possibility into such things that are no longer a possibility and are thus the impossible. It is one thing to just use the earth, another to receive the blessing of the earth and to become at home in the law of this reception in order to shepherd the mystery and watch over the inviolability of the possible. (Heidegger, 1987, p. 109)

"The inviolability of the possible" here is not commensurate with what we can do, assuming "that the human prerogative is unlimited, that we must do whatever we have the power to do. What is lacking (in such an assumption) is the idea that humans have a place and that this place is limited by responsibility on the one hand and by humility on the other." (Berry, 1983, pp. 54-55) Human action, human will, can, so to speak, spiral out of order, out of proportion, breaking the analogical threads of kinship that might delimit our prerogative. Our truly sane, human prerogative finds itself interwoven with the earth and the fundamental dependencies and reliances that "limit" our actions, not to what is conceivable but to what is sustainable.

The problem is, of course, that we can act without having a strong sense of where we are, of what reliances and harmonies "house" us (we can "leave"), and we often believe that this "can" is our freedom. Ecology (and pedagogy) remind us that if what we do despoils the conditions under which our doing can go on (if what we do befouls the earth which houses the possibility of doing anything), then such doings are not freedom but insanity. Such supposed "freedom" is insanity if it undercuts its own continuance, its own possibility.

Thus, ecology concerns not what we can do (in some Utopian sense which is literally no place), but what is proper, what is properly responsive to the place in which we find ourselves, those actions which have propriety, those which are "fitting," and which issue up out of a place as a considerate response to that place (i.e., a response that somehow acts in accordance with the sustainability of that response). Again, this language contains the notions of family resemblance and kinship. Being at home in a place. It requires action and thought which preserve the integrity of the place that houses us.

> Some people are beginning to try to understand where they are, and what it would mean to live carefully and wisely, delicately in place, in such a way that you can live there adequately and comfortably. Also, your children and grandchildren and generations a thousand years in the future would still be able to live there. That's living in terms of the whole fabric of living and life. (Snyder, 1980, p. 86)

The ecopedagogical response thus involves not just the possibility, but the necessity of returning, of renewal, and re-generativity.

> Reproduction is nurturing, patient, resigned to the pace of seasons and lives, respectful of the nature of things. Production's tendency is to go "all out"; it always aims to set a new record. Reproduction is more conservative and more modest; its aim is not to happen once, but to happen again and again and again, and so it seeks a balance between saving and spending. (Berry, 1986, p. 217)

Loving and savoring mathematics is preserving the ability to return to mathematics again and again and again. It involves preserving its generative, living character, shepherding its mystery. This means, put in the simplest fashion, that an understanding of mathematics involves attention to its integrities and dependencies and possibilities which draw us in again and again and again. It means that an understanding of mathematics which fails to open up the possibility of being drawn in again and again and again is, albeit unwittingly, self-degenerative. Its boundaries are unresonant, closed, fixed, allowing only the specialist to enter in. An understanding of mathematics which has no opening for and towards "the new ones" unwittingly cuts itself off from its own living sources; it breaks the kinships that house its own re-generation. It no longer knows where it is. It can thus believe that the mathematization of all things is not an act of befouling its own nest, but simply a consummation of its own indigenous destiny which needs nothing but itself in order to exist.

Living somewhere as if you and your children and their children will live there a thousand years is therefore not a matter of building impermeable edifices that will remain unchanged for a thousand years. It is a matter of building things that can be returned to, that are not "finished once and for all" but that are sustainable, repairable, modifiable, changeable, adaptable, re-interpretable, renewable, regenerable, able to be taken up anew again and again and again. To live carefully and wisely and delicately is to live such that this care and wisdom and delicacy can continue, and this sort of living-as-continuance already has room for children. More strongly put, such living is impossible without children, for without them a continuity of attention and devotion is impossible.

V

There is a peculiar etymological twist involved in the ability to do mathematics. It is the ability to "be at home with it." *Habilité*, inhabitation, being at home with something, being able. And being at home with something is being familiar, having familialness, finding family resemblances and kinships. And the parallel Sanskrit root of "kin" is *gen*: genesis, genealogy, generativity, generousness. Kin/kindness, generativity/generosity. Kindness and generosity. Affection, freely given.

VI

Where is our comfort but in the free, uninvolved, and finally mysterious beauty and grace of this world that we did not make, that has no price, that is not our work? Where is our sanity but here? Where is our pleasure but in working and resting kindly in the presence of this world? (Berry, 1988, p. 21)

In the end, our comfort is our strength. Resting kindly in the presence of the world is resting "in kind" or "with kindness." It is resting in those kinships, reliances, and dependencies, and cultivating the attention and devotion required, not to sever these reliances, but to sustain them, nurture them.

The peculiarity of ecopedagogical reflection is that it equates interdependency and reliance and indebtedness with comfort and strength and freedom. The resistance to such reflection is found in our inherited belief that we gain our strength in the severing of reliances and debts and dependencies. Descartes' *cogito ergo sum* is a perfect example of the impulse towards severance and the equation of truth with such severance and what follows from it. And, thinking we can live without "dependents" is precisely a closing out of children from our lives, and therefore a closing off of ourselves from the conditions of generativity and renewal.

The interweaving of ecology and pedagogy requires recovering a sense of faithfulness to these conditions, a sense of being true to the "finally mysterious beauty and grace of this world which we did not make." But this recovery must always be chosen anew and chosen again and again: mindfulness of our place on the earth is neither simple nor inevitable, nor achieved once and for all.

> Fidelity to human order, if it is fully responsible, implies fidelity also to natural order. Fidelity to human order makes devotion possible. Fidelity to natural order preserves the possibility of choice, the possibility of renewal of devotion. Where there is no possibility of choice, there is no possibility of faith. One who returns home, desiring anew what was previously chosen, is neither the world's stranger nor its prisoner, but is at once in place and free. (Berry, 1986, pp. 130-131)

But this passage makes these matters a little too grand. Our love and attention and devotion to the earth is always worked out in small and meticulous ways. The full weight of our ecological and pedagogical responsibility comes to bear here and here and here, in this next gesture, this next world. The kindliness and generosity of which it speaks is not a theory. It is borne out in how we live our lives on this precious earth.

Ecopedagogical reflection thus has two vital inseparable moments. It involves the deeply spiritual attention
required to be mindful of each gesture, each breath, and
the cherishing of the interdependencies and inevitabilities
that house us. It requires, in this sense, a phenomenology.
But it requires also an ability to read and become mindful
of the violations and compromises of such attention, of the
violences and severances out of which so much of our lives
and the lives of our children are built. It requires being
able to read these violations back into the linguistic, cultural, social, political, economic, and philosophical soil out
of which they have emerged. This, too, is our "everyday
life." This task, too, is a phenomenology. Without these
two moments, ecopedagogical reflection becomes a roman-
ticism that refuses to face where it actually is and the threads
of culpability that bind it here and here and here.

VII

My son took his mother out into our forest and asked,
in a matter-of-fact way, "Mom, this is my life tree. As long
as I live, it lives. When I die, it dies, and when it dies, I
die. Which one do you have, Mom?"

Coupling this with thoughts of the schooling he has in
store brings the horrible thought that he is bearing, for all
of us, the weight of a long-standing orientation to our earthly
lives that makes nonsense out of much of the life he actually lives.

This whole, longstanding edifice is brought down upon
his innocent doing of this little, meaningless mathematics
worksheet. He is bearing a schooled laughter on our be-

half, cut off so sharply and so easily from the deep belly laughs of springtime when he runs, unnamed and unnumbered, into the forest.

His unnamed bearing is ours and he will one day ask me what I've done.

But my hands are so full.

CHAPTER *Three*

THE SURROUNDINGS

I should be content
to look at a mountain
for what it is
and not as a comment
on my life.
(David Ignatow, 1980)

I

BEGINNING MEDITATION: There is a robin singing out straight south of our house, high up in one of the spruces or pines, out of sight but echoing off the hill to the west. Bursting full of the sunlight spring that has finally arrived after a terrible winter (dark cloud brain stem cabin fevers and all, wanting, at times, to scream out of my skin).

This is the third morning I've noticed him singing. He is there. But he is also there *again*. A brief little pitter-pattern, but not the sort of thing I'll report to others, because what would I say? How odd such saying would seem.

"Why are you telling me this?"

So, what is the character of such knowledge, and how does it differ from what usually passes as knowing?

How is such knowledge obtained?

What does such knowledge obtain? That is, what, precisely, is it that is known in such knowing? In these days of

37

meaning making (socially constructed or otherwise), can we tolerate believing that what is known here is, in any sense, *there*? Somehow *of* the earth *even if* I hadn't noticed? Can we imagine, in these days of hyper-consciousness, living as we academics do under the terrible burden of hyper-literacy, that human experience breaks out beyond the envelope of flesh? That such breaking out might not require a Foucaultian sadistic hyper-experience, but just might require quiet, rest, some attention spent to robins, some time spent beyond the confines of this weird, new, addictive God of post-modern urbanity?

How fragile, we might then ask, how long-lasting, how vital, how telling, is such a knowledge, not only of Robins and their habitualities, but of *that one*, *its* having returned, *there* up in *those* trees, in these failing days of May?

What is the goal of such knowing? What is it for? Where does it lead, and whom does it lead there?

What is the good of such knowledge? What good does it do to know this, and to pass it on in these written words?

What becomes of me in this sort of knowing? What becomes of me in attempting, here, to cite it in words on pages?

What does such knowing require of me in its obtaining, in its having and holding?

I'm sure I've experienced such robins before, but something, this time, is *striking* about having such experience.

Noticing that this pattern of living exists is odd enough.

Finding it, this time, so thrilling, is especially odd.

But there is something almost fearsome: finding that it is not only a noticing of patterns of robins, but a noticing *there*, of *that one*.

Noticing those things means conceding something else. If it is just there, just that one, then I am just here, just this one, in just this spring, under just this sun, and, after this horrible winter, feeling my age, feeling the passing of my days.

(Last fall, right in the middle of carrying wood in panic against the coming cold, something dropped. I will never finish this wood gathering. I will gather wood I gather. Then I will be dead. What a relief!)

I *feel* something in such knowing. It trickles out into the higher sun-arcs, into the clearing overhead, into the evidential bursts of living that are around me, the smell, the longings, the greenywhite plantdriven upwardness, spring. This knowing is, in part, a felt connectedness to all the small times humans have raised their heads and paused their breath and noticed the faces of the earth.

It is a felt connectedness to the way these yellow dandelions raise their heads to sunlight and turn and nod at its passing.

This one just this, and *that* one just that.

All the times of prayer over small foods, of thanksgiving and relief over sun's returning, of the bodily pleasures of fires from woodpiles cut and stored last summer. A sense of pleasure and gratitude and grace in hearing that Robin return, especially after this winter.

Deeply felt connection to all those hesitations.

Like the place of meditation, like the place of breath, this noticing is always *right where I left it.*

It is always The Same, even without my attention.

II

The smaller the surroundings become, the more vital and irreplaceable and necessary I seem to become to the character and continued existence of those surroundings. Not just smallness.

Speculation on theory and geography: that constructivism and its dark twin of deconstruction were born in the city, where I and others like me are rightly understood as vital and irreplaceable and necessary to such surroundings and their senses and significations and continuances. There, everything ultimately signifies us, as Makers of the World and constructivism and deconstruction orbit each other in the turns that are proper to that place.

III

Elbow River walk, winter 1997, -40 degrees Celsius, with icefog swirls rising up off the stillpatch water.

Brilliant Alberta Big Sun Blue Sky Blue. Past a low hill covered in three feet of snow. The unmistakable signs of a deer having humped its way down, two deep round fronthoof punctures and a huge ass-and-back-feet rumpprint, clunked downhill every four feet or so.

I have taken hundreds of these walks and never noticed such prints before.

This is so humiliating! *Where have I been?* And a cascade of feeling a sort of shame, a sort of nakedness before this hill, before this snow, before just these signs of just that deer, signified and now absent, and just me and no one else, with my own tracks trailed behind, standing here, stock still, breathing hard.

I sometimes so wish that these prints could just be prints and not a comment on my life. But as soon as they become deer prints, they point to what is absent, what is signified, and as soon as this first breakout appears, All Beings Innumerable show up to bear witness to these prints, my self included and this single life. Yes. These Beings Innumerable are a comment on my life and I don't really wish it otherwise.

So, where *have* I been? And how shall I answer these Beings Innumerable? How shall I repay the debts of my lack of attention, seen in the pretty rainbow oilslick oozing from the road overpass I've just driven to get here?

And who is this "I" that's been missing?

And how could it be that I could go missing in this way?

And what does all my writing rest upon with this gone unnoticed?

What are the geographies of these words you are reading?

Our epistemologies don't serve us especially well in such questions.

IV

> . . .the order and regularity in [what] we call nature, we ourselves introduce. We could never find [such orderliness and regularity]. . .had not we ourselves, or the nature of our mind, originally set them there. (Immanuel Kant, Critique of Pure Reason, 1767/1963, p. 147)

If order and regularity we ourselves introduce, without us the whole of things disassembles. Thus, theory and geography. A suspicion: deconstruction operates within the limits of human construction, *but there is no limit*, because, in Hegel's little horror show, any knowledge of such limits is always beyond such limits.

Hyperconsciousness: How could there be a world without us? And paranoia: What if there is!?

We could not find anything in the world if we had not put it there ourselves.

All knowledge is construction.

All intimacies are discoursed.

All care and love are simply hidden wills empowered.

All learning is caught in the sway of busi[y]ness.

All breath is measured.

All deadlines precisely that.

All reliance is slavery.

All naming is colonial.

All dependencies are to be treated with irony, cynicism, and condescension. (No longer three "R"s!)

Let's finally admit these as the real outcomes of post-modernism.

Perhaps these moods are not necessary to post-modernism. Perhaps it is not depression. Perhaps it is not cabin fever.

But it must find more of a belly heaved beneath its crown of words.

I need more of a belly heaving beneath my crowns of words.

V

A sweet friend took a group of people up into the Rocky Mountains, and sat them in a circle, enticing them, in an ecological exercise, to breath this place, to recollect themselves and their relations, here, to "re-connect."

A sudden muffled *CA-COOM* of heavy pawprints lifted off a low spruce up the hill above their heads.

Cougar.

And the footloose giddy rockstumble run and fast as possible that resulted. And in the puffy airgasp, in the bloodypump redness, in the nickelspittle of mouths dried to tears, belly laughs of a deeply felt and fearsome connectedness that had broken the spell of heady thoughts of Mother earth.

Edibility.

Here, then, sits the fallacy, but it is no longer an epistemological fallacy. It is no longer a quarrel about concepts and subjects and objects and patterns and schemata and structures and where they are located and who is who and what belongs to which.

Surely we all bring our lives to bear on what we see, how we live, what we think, how and when the heart warms.

Just as surely, we "construct"—that is, we "make" something of—what comes to meet us.

And just as surely, the paw thumps of that cougar were "read" as "signs" of "something."

But it is not a significance we can endlessly postpone at our leisure, toying with it, and finally hating it for its obviousness.

Crawling underneath these sureties is the certain knowledge that these makings are also *the problem* we face in our humanity.

The chattering monkey is always narrating, so that any attempt to rest in the ways of things and to allow what is beyond us to have *its own* ways, *its own* dharma, is haunted by the bareteethed chitter-who-who-who of this is this and that is that and what if and when and then and therefore.

Monkey mind.

And a bit of a hint about the geographies of these theories I hold so dear.

VI

I just imagine the cynical postmodernist caught and felled by that cougar. And as its teeth begin to pull bloody human thigh muscles from their place, we see the final grinning sneer at the cougar for being so *obvious*, so *foundationalist*, so bereft of the twittery insight that my leg might not signify food at all! Ha ha!

VII

I'm not sure if this is a dream: Walking to Lakeshore Public School through the powerline field in spring just after a big rain, and seeing the trembly beginning of a small stream, big elementary-school-yellow-Crayola sun, big blue smile of sky, and moist, fleshy eye-corner water runoff snaking through the newly-lifted white brightygreen blades.

Today, spring runoff trailing through aspens that have just opened and cast green parabolas under the sun's airblue arch over foothills. Yes! Sunlight and the teeth of lions.

Entering the powers and potentialities of this place through damming up water with sticks, or cutting shoeslide mudtroughs for letting water flowfaster.

Damming and letting go. A swinging gate.

Down on my hands and knees forty-six years old (just got a soaker!) prodding at the sticks holding the organic bubbly surfacefroth of fastrunning overflow stream wanting to feel the breathrush of release working to no end then squatting, sunshine, meditation, breathmeasures, after, hard, walk, in, fog, steaming, up, off, weeks of woody rain.

Fatsquat. Bellytilt. Breath. Looking upstream and

knowing that something was slowly coming down stream out of the yellowy lightturns of water.

Close to awe.

Not awe of the eyes and brains and ascendancy and visions. Eyes drawn down. The crawly awe of muscles and shit and wormy earth smells.

Just around those little bends.

Coming this way.

Under the purposeless warbles of robin halos overhead.

CHAPTER *Four*

"LITTERED
WITH LITERACY"

An Ecopedagogical Reflection
on Whole Language, Pedocentrism,
and the Necessity of Refusal

Prelude: On "Ecopedagogy"

> No matter the distinctions we draw, the connections,
> the dependencies, remain. To damage the earth is to
> damage your children. (Wendell Berry, The Unsettling
> of America)

THE TERM "ECOPEDAGOGY" is meant to re-awaken
a sense of the intimate interconnection between ecological
awareness and pedagogy. This interconnection is not the
outcome of a concerted application of the principles and
practices of one domain (ecology) to another domain (pedagogy). Such questions of "domains" and "application" between ecology and pedagogy inadvertently assume the separation of these two disciplines, and assume, as well, that
somehow the connections between the sustainable
generativities of the earth and the generativity represented
by children and embraced by pedagogy are somehow ours
to be made, not made or unmade. As the above-cited passage from Berry suggests, such matters are not at our dis-

posal or discretion to connect or disconnect. More point-edly, these matters are not at our disposal to ignore under the guise of "working in another area." Even, say, in the realm of the mathematics curriculum, ecopedagogical im-ages and profound ecological consequences and choices have already been made and are always already at work (Jardine, 1990).

Ecopedagogy assumes that there is always and already a deep, ambiguous kinship at work between the real, earthly life of children, the tasks of pedagogy (including our un-derstandings of various curriculum specializations, how we envisage and practice a relation between the old and the young, our conceptions and embodiments of knowledge, and our images of ourselves and our tasks as teachers) and the earth's "limits of necessity and mystery" (Berry, 1983, p. 13). This ambiguous kinship can be simply framed, although its implications pose enormous questions to our lives as pedagogues and to the telling tales that underlie our practices:

♦ To the extent that ecology considers the conditions under which life can go on (Smith, 1988a), it is always already intimately pedagogic at its heart.

♦ To the extent that the task of pedagogy is to usher children into those understandings of the Earth's ways re-quired for life to go on in a full and healthy and wholesome and sustainable way, it is already intimately ecological at its heart.

Finally, at the heart of the notion of ecopedagogy hides a traumatic twist. It is possible to work with full confi-dence and fully gracious intent in the area of pedagogy, and yet betray an unintended ecological insanity. We can speak with grand aspirations of our hopes for our children while remaining unaware of how those very aspirations, in their ecological assumptions and consequence, might work against the actual breath required to utter them. We can do the impossible.

Ecopedagogy and the Unsustainable Extremities of Language Arts Curriculum

These broad formulations of the nature of ecopedagogy can be particularized to various curricular areas in the following way: what constitutes, for example, a sustainable and generative understanding of the ways of language and texts and reading and writing?

Such an understanding of language curriculum must consider both how new growth can be nurtured, encouraged, and sustained, and what must be conserved/preserved of the old growth and the old rooting soils for this nurturance, encouragement, and sustenance to remain possible. Language curriculum theories and practices must not become too enamored of the new and the young, or we may lose sight of the conditions under which the new can thrive. Such theories and practices must not become too enamored of the old, or we might lose sight of the ways in which the old requires the fecund re-generativity and transformation that the young provide.

In the area of language arts curriculum, we have tended to "ride the pendulum" between these extremities in search of a clear and solid and fixed foundation for our theories and practices. Ecology suggests, however, that there is no such securable ground to the living practices of human

Littered with Literacy

life, only ongoing, shifting, ambiguous nests or communities of interrelations which are constantly in need of re-newal, re-generation, re-thinking. And this suggests that in the area of pedagogy:

> The old unilateral options of gericentrism (appealing to the authority of age, convention, tradition, nostalgia) and pedocentrism (child-centered pedagogy) only produce monstrous states of siege which are irresponsible to the matters at hand, i.e., to the question of how life is mediated through relations between the old and young. (Smith, 1988, p. 176)

Human life thrives only in this "belly of a paradox" (Smith, 1988, p. 175)—the ongoing nests of interrelations between the old and the young, the established and the new. Both gericentrism and pedocentrism can thus be understood as breakdowns in this living nest or community of relations—attempts to anchor educational theory or practice to a fixed point (e.g., "the child is the center of the curriculum" or "back to basics") instead of in the mediated set of relations themselves. The child at the center will always have to confront what is basic in curriculum if it is truly basic to the course of human life; what is basic in curriculum will always have to be understandable to the child, invigorating of their life, and invigorated by their taking it up anew. Out of relation, both of these extremities become monstrous.

Healthy language arts theories and practices must consider how to embrace this continuously mediated and remediated state of interdependency that inheres in the living nature of language itself and how to become tolerant of the difficulty and ambiguity that inheres in it (and this in spite of the fact that a certain clarity and cleanness would result if we simply severed these interdependencies and fell prey to either gericentrism or pedocentrism). The life of language occurs in the tensive, mediated interplays between the forms and disciplines and established wisdoms of/in language and the newly erupting voices of the young. These extremities *depend upon one another*, and each finds both its (re)source and its limit in its opposite. Without the renewal that the young provide (Arendt, 1969, p. 187), the senatorial (e.g., a piece of literature considered by the wisdoms of age and convention and tradition to be worthwhile, a piece of literature that is thus ripe for re-consideration, open and ready to support and nurture and teach the young) can become simply the senile (e.g., already fixed and established answers in the back of the book which foreclose on the necessity of children ever needing to deeply consider this work, since the "answers" seem to be already on hand, not needing their consideration). Similarly, without the deep rooting soils that age and time and wisdom and discipline provide, the beautiful voice of the individual child (e.g., the child as author/originator [Harste, Short, & Burke 1988, p. 5]) can end up merely puerile. Put more colloquially, the young and the old are dependents, kin, relations/related, and only *in* these relations does each avoid its weakest aspect (senility, puerility). Each finds comfort (common fortitude, strength) in the other.

Rather than attempting to *solve* this precarious and tensive interplay between the old/established and the young/new, healthy and sustainable language arts theories and practices attempt to bear this ambivalence in the understanding that "ambivalence is the adequate reaction to the whole truth" (Hillman, 1987, p. 15) about language as a living system. The task then is not to solve this ambivalence, but to resolve ourselves to "make meaningful and beautiful th[is] primary paradox that human beings *have* to live with" (Snyder, 1980, pp. 29-30).

Understood this way, what at first appears to be a failure to finally and once and for all figure out the language arts curriculum for young children in a solid and fixed and clear fashion, complete with a consistent and comprehensible theory and a package of fail-safe, teacher- and child-proof practices—this apparent failure just might turn out to be our greatest success. It may signal a glimmer of the deeply (inter)dependent life of language that goes beyond our desires for fixity and clarity and centration (the central urges of literalism). Accountable and warrantable action in the language arts classroom always *depends*. It must proceed as a living response to the living, deeply dependent interactions that pertain in that classroom. This child's work may call for a more honed and careful attention to some of the disciplines of language; that child may need to be encouraged to be more free and ebullient in writing; it may be the appropriate time to introduce these children to that author. And all of these actions are never necessarily accountable in all cases, as if what is needed in order to write well never *depends* on the living relations in which each child finds him- or herself immersed.

This may *appear* to be child centered, but it is neither this nor its opposite. Warrantable action does not depend only on the child, but, for example, on the child's ability to communicate to this audience in that fashion about these topics. Thus, we are always confronted with the child *in relation* to the disciplines and conventions of communication, *in relation* to the varieties of audience (to which writing must be obedient—*ab audire*: audience and obedience are rooted together etymologically), *in relation* to this type of writing (e.g., a letter) and its forms and features, and *in relation* to these topics which have probably already been written about in a myriad of ways (ways which themselves bespeak a myriad of relations)—and all of this *in relation* to what the child has already come to understand about these matters, *in relation* to the classroom setting and the tasks currently underway. Although the child surely figures strongly in all these relations, he or she is not the "center" of these relations except in the most porous of senses. Sometimes, for example, the demands of convention will decenter the child, demanding that he or she learn more or differently. Sometimes, for example, convention will say "no" to the child—gently, one hopes, with care and tact, full of pedagogic intent, but "no" nevertheless. This "no" is an attempt to keep the child *in relation*, to keep him or her rooted in the dependencies needed to sustain his or her ongoing, generative efforts. This "no," this refusal, is thus not precisely *against* the child, but is rather against allowing, in the name of the child and of the generativity he or she brings, the despoilment of the conditions under which the child's ongoing, generative efforts can sustainably continue.

In this way, language arts becomes a delicate, ambiguous, ecological matter.

"Littered with Literacy": The Ecologies of Whole Language

Whole language can be understood as an effort aimed at "restoring [the] life [of language] to its original difficulty" (Caputo, 1987)—the original difficulty that pertains in its deep and generative state of (inter)dependency. This attempt to restore generative relations, dependencies, connections, is also an ecological effort in its premise and consequence. It is thus no coincidence that the continuing growth of interest in whole language is occurring now, in the midst of a growing interest in ecological issues of wholeness and health. Ecology reminds us that the earth is a living system constituted by a vast interweaving and interconnected web of dependencies. To live well on the earth is to learn to live in and with these dependencies. After all, as Wendell Berry (1977, p. 14) suggests:

> the care of the earth is our most ancient and most worthy and, after all, our most pleasing responsibility. To cherish what remains of it, and to foster its renewal, is our only legitimate hope.

Likewise, whole language tells us that the vibrancy and life of language is found in its living interdependencies, not in its lifeless fragments (writing cut off from reading, phonics or graphics cut off from meaning, authorship and originality cut off from discipline, ebullience cut off from craft, and the like). A pedagogy that is becoming of such interdependencies is likewise "our only legitimate hope," and the "continuity of attention and devotion" (Berry, 1977, p. 14) that such a pedagogy requires cannot help but be "our most pleasing responsibility." This perhaps bespeaks the deep pleasure and relief expressed by many teachers upon their introduction to whole language—a "release" of sorts into the living beauty of language as lived, and a freedom from its deadening calcifications. This is not the pleasure of triviality and ease and simplicity: it is the pleasure of coming upon "the real work" (Snyder, 1980) of language and its real "original difficulty."

Framed in this way, it is clear how "whole language" is not offering yet another theory about language or another "method" (Newman, 1985). Whole language wishes to turn our attention to how it is that we *already live* in language. As with ecological awareness, what is at stake is not a *theory*. It is our living that is at stake: how we actually live in the world (of language) and what such living requires of us if it is to be sustainable and healthy and whole. What is first and foremost is not some clear and consistent theory, but the real, living practices of living readers and writers in the world (Edelsky, Altwerger, & Flores, 1991, p. 22; Harste, Short, & Burke, 1988, p. 3) with all the contradiction, paradox, and living difficulty that such a world requires and invites.

It is no coincidence, then, that Constance Weaver (1990, p. 106) uses ecological metaphors to describe the character of a whole language classroom:

The classrooms are "littered with literacy": that is, they offer a rich variety of environmental print as well as books, magazines, and newspapers. They are print-rich environments.

We have here a wonderful image of a classroom bursting full of language in all its living forms. This image works against a certain old image of cleanness (an image often linked to clarity—see Jardine, 1992, pp. 31-51; Turner, 1987, p. 7) and evokes an "untidy," ambiguous, earthy sense in which "litter" is a necessary precondition of healthy growth. Ecologically speaking, such a littered language classroom is not organized to suit some need *other than* this living world of language itself (e.g., ease of institutional/logico-mathematical accountability—one could consider the clarity and cleanness of a phonics worksheet and the "mess" created by linking phonics back to *this* child's desire to communicate well about *this* topic to *this* friend or enemy). Such a littered classroom is, however, very orderly, oriented to the indigenous orderliness of the living world of language itself: in the *life* of language, phonemic and graphic conventions exist on behalf of making communication with others more "convenient." The mastery of such conventions does not disappear in the whole language classroom. On the contrary, such conventions are re-generated and re-enlivened by being linked back to the living reasons for such mastery. Such mastery makes a difference in how we can live (in language). Whole language names this living order of a living system and the whole language classroom is thus constituted by *living in* this order.

This is a deeply ecological sense of "littered with literacy": the sense in which, for example, trees spontaneously litter every year. The material which trees regularly scatter around is precisely that which is required to sustain the tree itself and sustain the possibility of producing new life. In and through littering, it is building its own humus and even in the passing of this particular tree, its own "death becomes potentiality" (Berry, 1983, p. 73) as it adds its own life to the conditions for the possibility of new life.

Here is an image for understanding the community established in the whole language classroom (Calkins, 1986; Harste, Short, & Burke, 1988; Graves, 1983) as an ecosystem in which:

> the community is an order of memories preserved consciously in instructions, songs and stories, and both

consciously and unconsciously in ways. A healthy culture holds preserving knowledge in place for a long time. That is, the essential wisdom accumulates in the community much as fertility builds in the soil. (Berry, 1983, p. 73)

The litter of literacy in such a classroom allows children and teachers alike to learn the ways of language by generatively participating in and contributing to these ways. Such a classroom is constituted by the interplays between the generativity and liveliness and authority/originality of the young and the ways and stories and order of memories needed to sustain such generativity. Whole language requires envisaging language, not as an inert set of instruments that are at our beck and call, but as something that houses us, something we are in, something which responds to us and something to which we are responsible. We are "in" the community of language. And once we envisage language as a place in which we dwell, the emphasis of whole language on "communication" becomes immediately obvious, communication being the generative case of community. Also, understood as a "community," language is understood to have a life and a history and a wisdom that both goes beyond the individual and that needs the individual ("the new blood," to use an archaic term common to the initiation of the new ones into the community) for its own renewal. As a sustainable community or place, it includes both the old/established and the young/new and provides a place for each to find its source and limit, its comfort, in the other.

The hidden ecological irony in the use of the notion "littered with literacy" should not be ignored, however, because it signals a potentially dangerous misunderstanding of whole language. "Littered with literacy" is *intended* to signal richness, fullness, and diversity. But it also evokes images of consumption and disposal, abandonment, excess and irresponsibility. "Litter" in this more colloquial sense suggests a loss of a sense of memory and place. Whole language can easily be confused with a form of *pedocentrism* and with a sort of linguistic free-for-all that at best ignores and at worst despises age, tradition, convention, discipline, and the like. Believing this cracks apart the sustainable community of language and ushers in the potential of monstrous states of siege—or, better, pedocentrism is an all too appropriate metaphor for a monstrous educational community which "leaves children to their own devices." Even more strongly put, Arendt suggests that such a community is constituted by "abandonment and betrayal." (Arendt, 1969, pp. 188, 196)

Let us look at the roots of this misconstrual of whole language as a form of pedocentrism. If we consider the whole language classroom as a place where children might be at home in language, consider the following passage in relation to Weaver's description of her classroom:

> It is impossible to divorce the question of what we do from the question of where we are—or, rather, where we think we are. That no sane creature befouls its own nest is accepted as generally true. What we conceive to be our nest, and where we think it is, are therefore questions of the greatest importance. (Berry, 1986, p. 51)

A classroom "littered with literacy" must be understood as a living place, a nest. The question then becomes one of how to resist the sense of "litter" that suggests befouling this nest. There is a sense in which a classroom can become all too easily "littered" with garbage that does not lend itself to the life of language in its wholeness and health and that therefore (intentionally or not) works against an environment which will sustain and nurture the young. A nest works against itself if it becomes too centered on the young; it is properly and sustainably "centered" on the bearing and nurturing and protecting and teaching and raising and attending to the portends of the young. It is thus not precisely "centered" but "decenterd" outwards into ecopedagogical relations between the young and the ways of raising, the young and the limits of protecting, the young and the teachings, and so on. And these relations are always such that, for example, the teachings will tell us something about the young, but the young, too, will tell us something about the teachings. Each will invigorate and strengthen the other. This is the sense is which ecology is understandably conservative in one sense (wishing to conserve the conditions under which life can go on) and not conservative in another (realizing that those conditions require the regeneration, renewal, revision, transformation that the young provide). These "relations," if they are healthy, are always right in the midst of being re-thought, re-newed, re-established. The ongoing "conversation" between the old/established and the young/new is thus not an error. What is an error is not allowing this conversation to go on in a healthy way. "Garbage" is what works against this nest of relations by existing "out of relation": garbage is always "out of place."

"No sane creature befouls its own nest." If we look again at this example of the littering tree, it becomes evident how we are unlike it. For the most part, the tree cannot work against its own sustenance and renewal. It cannot "litter" in the sense of producing garbage. Unlike the tree, we are possessed of what at first glance appears to be a certain freedom. We, unlike the tree, can do the impossible:

> The unnoticeable law of the earth preserves the earth in the sufficiency of the emerging and perishing of all things in the allotted sphere of the possible which everything follows and yet nothing knows. The birch tree never oversteps its possibility. It is [human] will which drives the earth beyond the sphere of its possibility into such things that are no longer a possibility and are thus the impossible. It is one thing to just use the earth, another to receive the blessing of the earth and to become at home in the law of this reception in order to shepherd the mystery and watch over the inviolability of the possible. (Heidegger, 1987, p. 109)

Human action, human will, can, so to speak, spiral out of order, out of proportion, breaking the earthly "limits of necessity and mystery" that might delimit our prerogative to what is ecologically possible (i.e., to what is sustainable). Our truly sane, human prerogative is not commensurate with what we *can* do, assuming

> that the human prerogative is unlimited, that we must do whatever we have the power to do. What is lacking [in such an assumption] is the idea that humans have a place and that this place is limited by responsibility on the one hand and by humility on the other. (Berry, 1983, pp. 54-5)

Simply filling a classroom with all possible forms of

print and allowing any and every form of language arts activity assumes that everything we *can* fill the classroom with is "litter" and not "garbage." However, as a practiced teacher knows, littering the classroom with literacy names a profound nest of *decisions* on the part of the teacher, decisions taken in full awareness that we can do the impossible. Because we can do the impossible, we must understand the deep interrelations that inhere in the wholeness and health of language and we must refuse that which might violate or overstep those limits—that which would turn litter into garbage. And this knowledge must be held with a delicateness and openness that allows the young to rise up and take issue with what we think we know of these matters. "Knowledge of these limits and how to live within them is the most comely and graceful knowledge that we have, the most healing and the most whole." (Berry, 1986, p. 94) And, to be comely and graceful, this knowledge needs the arrival of the young and the re-vivifying they bring to such knowing. Such knowledge is had only by the teacher him- or herself living in the midst of language as a real writer, a real reader, someone attuned both to how language responds to us and how we are responsible to it. Under the surface gloss of occasional "relentless enthusiasm," (Smith, 1988b, p. 236) the whole language teacher develops a deep and considered sense of restraint that is gained from living well in the interior of language itself and nurturing in oneself such comely and graceful knowledge, holding it in place for a long time and *living with the consequences* (Berry, 1986, 1983). This is the living, generative sense of the restraint that inheres in dependents/dependence/(inter)relations. "By restraint they make themselves whole." (Berry, 1986, p. 95)

Whole Language and the Necessity of Refusal

North American culture is not one especially enamoured of restraint or dependence, born as it is out of unearthly, metaphysical images of freedom and independence. And it is important to consider how whole language was itself born in part as a response to earlier language arts practices which suppressed the individual's desire to write under the weight of the disciplines of language. In its first flush, it is too easy to imagine that whole language involves the overturning of such weight and the unabashed acceptance and confirmation of everything and anything without restraint, without limit or measure, without disciplined and considered refusal. It does not. And to believe so is to confuse whole language with pedocentrism. There is, however, a sense in which whole language easily lends itself to such confusion. Again, the lessons of ecology are telling in this regard.

There has been a disturbing loss in the area of ecological awareness. Currently, in Canada at least, there are three "R"s to environmentalism: reduce, reuse, and recycle (some have introduced a fourth "R": recover). Several years ago there was another, different fourth "R" which has since gone missing: refuse.

It is vital to not misread this missing fourth "R." It is not simply "refuse" in the sense of "garbage." It also suggests refusal. The most potent form of ecological action is simply saying "no" to those elements of our lives and our ways that are unsustainable, that befoul our nest. Saying 'no' to the garbage. Refusing. The loss of this fourth "R"—the loss of the power and potency and responsibility involved in the act of refusal—is, unfortunately, not very mysterious. It leaves us with a vision of ecology which does not demand that we take responsibility for our own consumptive desires except *after* they are fully satiated. We can consume anything we want as long as we deal with the garbage *afterwards*. We are not required to consider how it may be that much of what we consume is *itself* garbage and how our relentless consumptiveness—our inability to say "no"—might itself spell ecological disaster. We live in an economy geared to saying "yes" without hesitation, geared to growth without restraint, geared to the giddy sense of consumptive vitality that such a headlong rush provides.

In a horrible twist of logic, the relinquishing of the power of refusal leads to precisely that sense of rootlessness and powerlessness and futility that makes one susceptible to becoming a relentless consumer who is unable to refuse:

> People whose governing habit is the relinquishment of power, competence and responsibility, and whose characteristic suffering is the anxiety of futility, make excellent spenders. They are the ideal consumers. By inducing in them little panics of boredom, powerlessness, sexual failure, mortality, paranoia, they can be made to buy virtually anything that is "attractively packaged." (Berry, 1986, p. 24)

I cannot help but read this passage in relation to the lurid advertisements that haunt educational magazines, offering purchasable whole language kits and packages for instant classroom use. In an almost inevitable turn, whole language has become "the latest thing," purchasable and consumable with, it seems, little cost, little agony, and little real work:

> Dr. Terry Johnson will show you (quickly and easily) how to turn your classroom into a whole language

64 Littered with Literacy

showplace. You'll learn everything you need to know to profoundly increase your whole language teaching skills (And. . .we'll even buy you lunch!) (Johnson, 1990, p. 32)

As with ecology, however, whole language at its heart works against this unsustainable "modernism" and its giddy, puerile enamorment with the easily and quickly consumable:

What we call the modern world is not necessarily, and not often, the real world, and there is no virtue in being up-to-date in it. It is a false world, based upon economies and values and desires that are fantastical—a world in which millions of people have lost any idea of the materials, the disciplines, the restraints, and the work necessary to support human life, and have thus become dangerous to their own lives and to the possibility of life. The job now is to get back to that perennial and substantial world in which we really do live, in which the foundations of our life will be visible to us, and in which we can accept our responsibilities again within the conditions of necessity and mystery. (Berry, 1983, p. 13)

Whole language evokes this archaic, ecological sense of the perennial and substantial world of language as lived (a world, of course, full of vivid uprisings of "the new, the different, the true" [Gadamer, 1977, p. 51])—a world which is not quick, not easy, not constituted by the surface fashionabilities (and rapid outdatability) of a showplace and in which one *never* learns everything they need to know. Against a comely and graceful knowledge of the life and limits of language, we are able to refuse the giddy fantasy versions of "whole language" that in fact despoil it. Whole language, as a way of living in language (and therefore precisely *not* as an easily purchasable and consumable thing), provides a way to say no, to refuse in a strong and considered way.

So here is the rub. In its first flush, whole language found itself out from under the gericentric senile anonymity of work sheets, lovingly ushering the ebullient child into the heart of language. But in this adrenaline rush of vigor into language arts practices, we can too easily confuse this influx of vigor with unabashed pedocentrism. Consider the case of a ten-year-old boy who, in response to the question, "Are you a good writer?" says. "I don't know. My teacher says everything is good." As Lucy Calkins (1986, p. 165) warns, "Out of fear of 'taking ownership' [we can] desperately avoid teaching." This timidity is what Hannah Arendt (1969, p. 181) calls the feeling of "standing helpless before the child," the sense of being "out of relation", having "relinquished our identities as teachers in order to give students ownership of their craft" (Calkins, 1986, p. 165). The teacher who says that "everything is good," even if they do so in the name of confirming the child, displays, however unwittingly, a lack of the knowledge of language and its traditions that might make considered resistance possible and generative for the child. By being unable (or unwilling) to considerately and tactfully and delicately refuse, the child is abandoned to his or her own devices. Worse still, this child is abandoned in the full knowledge that the teacher's relentless confirmations are simply garbage. And, finally, with no good example of considered refusal, the child is not taught how to say "no" for him- or herself to the unsustainable garbage that surrounds him. This is not *whole* language, and its supporters must avoid the allure of such grinning enthusiasm. Whole language does not require such timidity in the face of the child.

Not surprisingly, with this relinquishing of the power of refusal, we also relinquish any strong and considered sense of acceptance. I recall reading the first few pages of *A Wizard of Earthsea* (Le Guin, 1968) to a group of elementary school teachers and the turmoil caused when the suggestion was made that it was a good book, worthy of the attention of children and adults, strong and well-drawn in its characters, and so on. Again, this turmoil suggests a sort of timidity and rootlessness: in the name of affirming everyone's right to their own opinion, all opinions about a text are equally "uprooted" and therefore none can be strongly affirmed as a good opinion of the text. Once the power of refusal is relinquished, any notion of a good or strong opinion, one that "stands" becomes understandable only as the *disconfirmation* of the individual and their right to *their own* opinion. We become unable to voice any strong preference for Le Guin's book because preference becomes scattershot into always and only *personal* preference. In such a context, whole language easily blurs out into a type of expressionist rhetoric of "private visions" and "personal opinions" (Berlin, 1988) which are always only directed towards affirming themselves ("this is my opinion": whole language confused with *self-affirmation*). This results in the puerile and ecologically disastrous belief that nothing *pertains* beyond the individual and his or her "personal preferences." Just as we can easily abandon and betray children by leaving them to their own devices, this despoiling of Ursula Le Guin's work in the name of children and their right to their own opinions abandons and betrays the world by saying, in this case, that any possible opinion, (and hence nothing in particular) pertains to it. Here, Le

Guin's work is not allowed to have the power of refusal, the power of saying "no" to certain opinions. Again, this is not *whole* language.

In this way, then, the loss of the ability to refuse is twinned with the loss of the ability to accept. Against these twin timidities, whole language wishes to recover a strong sense of refusal and acceptance. It does not wish to do so according to some geriphilic notion of law and order, nor to some pedophilic fantasy of the preciousness of the young, but through a strong and vital and vibrant sense of community and a sense in which that community needs the new blood of the young. This necessitates a strong sense of our dual responsibility as teachers:

> Education is the point at which we decide whether we love the world enough to assume responsibility for it and by the same token, save it from the ruin which, except for renewal, except for the coming of the new and the young, would be inevitable. And education, too, is where we decide whether we love our children enough not to expel them from our world and leave them to their own devices. (Arendt, 1969, p. 196)

Only in this ambivalent twinning of responsibilities is the life of language possible in its wholeness.

Concluding Reflections

Gericentrism wars against the wildness of youth and pedocentrism rails against the calcifications of age. In such states of siege, each extreme reads its opposite in its weakest aspect. Whole language can be conceived as an effort directed towards the mending and healing of these besieged relations. It wishes to read these opposites in relation to each other, and therefore to read each in its strength. As such, whole language is a deeply ecological phenomenon. But, as with ecology, there is a sting to this issue. It is my own wholeness and health that it at issue in whole language. Differently put, to understand language in its wholeness, it must be taken up "from the inside."

Ecopedagogical reflection places the issue of language arts theories and practices back into the sphere in which we actually live—the sphere of my understanding and care and attention to language, my love of good books and good writing, my joy at the ebullience of children's work and the hard work they can pursue in the name of communication/community, my patience and frustration and their (and my own) occasional puerility and lack of discipline and care, the wisdom and originality they can display, and the pleasures that can come from delving into the wisdoms of the world and measuring one's life against them, learning from them. Ecopedagogical reflection places the issue of language back into the writing of this very paper and the gericentrisms and pedocentrisms to which it may have fallen prey.

Ecopedagogy in the area of language arts practices inevitably centers the "continuity of attention and devotion" (Berry, 1986, p. 14) that a generative and deep understanding of writing and reading and texts requires *of me* and *of the life I actually live (in language)*. Such attention and devotion is not a trick or method or technique: it is a form of *life* dedicated to developing a deep sense of the wholeness and health of language and therewith developing my own wholeness and health *in* language. Because I can do the impossible, such wholeness and health requires that I develop a strong (and generative) and considered (and considerate) sense of acceptance and refusal.

CHAPTER *Five*
"THE STUBBORN PARTICULARS OF GRACE"

Prelude

CANADIAN POET Bronwen Wallace entitled her third collection of poems *The Stubborn Particulars of Grace* (1987). Reference to this title comes up in a poem called "Particulars" which is full of the meticulous details of memory and reverie ("those Sundays at my grandmother's table") and which shows the way that our lives are always lived right here, in the face of these stubborn particulars. Wallace's work gains its deep resonances, its sense of wholeness, not through nebulous talk of grand things, but because it consistently "argue[s] the stubborn argument of the particular, right now, in the midst of things, *this* and *this*" (p. 111).

This stubborn argument of the particular is reminiscent of a fragment of William Carlos Williams' *Spring and All* (1923/1991, p. 224):

So much depends
upon
the red wheel
barrow

glazed with rain
water
beside the white
chickens.

Here, an ordinarily insignificant object is portrayed with
such spacious clarity that the insight becomes unavoidable: somehow, *everything* depends upon this red wheelbarrow. Somehow, a mindfulness to "*this* and *this*," the particular object, in its very particularity, becomes like a sacred place where the whole earth comes to nestle in relations of deep interdependency.

This is one of the secrets of ecological mindfulness. To
understand what is right in front of us in an ecologically
sane, integrated way is to somehow see this particular thing
in place, located in a patterned nest of interdependencies
without which it would not be what it is. Differently put,
"understanding 'the whole'" involves paying attention to
this "in its wholeness." This rootedness in the particular
is what helps prevent ecology from becoming woozy and
amorphous—a disembodied idea that misses the particularities in the flit of *this* ruby-crowned kinglet pair in the
lower pine branches and how this movement is so fitting
here, in the coming arch of spring in the Rocky Mountain
foothills.

Math Facts on a Teddy Bear's Tummy

During practicum supervision in a Grade One classroom over the past year, I witnessed again a common sight.
The children are in the middle of a "bear theme." In order
to integrate with this theme and in order to make the work

"more fun for the kids" (as one teacher put it), mathematics addition facts are printed on the stomach of a cut-out line drawing of a teddy bear.

Such "activities"—where the mathematics questions are answered and the bears are colored in and posted on the wall of the classroom—are certainly carried out with the best of intentions. Blaming teachers for engaging their children in such trite activities in the name of "curriculum integration" belies the fact that we are *all* "witnessing the inevitable outcome of a logic [of fragmentation, severance, and dis-integration] that is already centuries old and that is being played out in our own lifetime" (Berman, 1983, p. 23). More strongly put, we are all, however unwittingly, *living out this logic.* Teachers, children, administrators, university academics—we have all, in our own ways, been victimized by the uprootedness and "unsettling" (Berry, 1986) caused by this logic. Such classroom activities should therefore not be taken up as occasions for blame, but as interpretive opportunities that give us all ways to address how we might make our pedagogical conduct more integrated and whole.

What we see occurring with these math facts on a teddy bear's tummy is what could be called an "urban sprawl" version of integration. To integrate one subject area with another, one begins with the clear, unambiguous, univocal, literal surfaces features of a particular activity (for example, "5+3=__" as a so-called "math fact") and moves laterally, adding more and more (clear, unambiguous, univocal, literal surface feature) activities from different subject areas. We can hear in teacher's talk such as "I wanted to make the math stuff more fun for the children by linking it up to things they were already doing" the understandable desire to rescue "5+3=__" from its flatness and isolation.

Understood and presented merely as a "math fact," it is rather severe, so we find ways to remedy this malady by "dressing it up" through combining it with cut-out line drawings of bears (which the children supposedly find cute and interesting).

The problem, however, is that such integration (if one could call it that) works precisely because it operates with the thinnest veneer of each area. Curricular integration becomes akin to formulations of post-modernism which so well describe the mood of so many elementary schools: a hyperactive play of surfaces juxtaposed at the whim of "the subject" (whether teacher or child), juxtaposable with facile ease precisely because we are dealing with uprooted surfaces which offer no real resistance and demand no real work. Integration in such a post-modern milieu becomes formulated as little more than surface co-presence or co-occurrence, bereft of any fleshy, experiential immediacy.

If we begin with a surface understanding of "5+3=___" our efforts at integration can easily fall prey to the bizarre cultural-capitalist equation of the achievement of wholeness with the consumptive accumulation of "more." One makes "5+3=___" (or any other curricular fragment) "whole," not by sticking with it, deepening it, opening up its "necessities and mysteries" (Berry, 1983, p. vii) but by adding more and more activities to it—surrounding and crowding it with other equally isolated, unopened particulars but, we might say, never "housing" it. In this way, to re-formulate Wendell Berry's (1986) critique of the motto of the Sierra Club, our interest in "math facts" become *scenic*, something to "do," like, say, "doing" the Grand Canyon. Mathematics becomes akin to a tourist attraction, something to look at but never enter into, open up and learn to live with well. And we, in turn, become akin to curricular tourists, ready to be momentarily entertained and amused. However, since we just see the thin, tarted-up, presentable surface of things, we, along with our children, become equally subject to boredom, frustration, and eventual violence. Given what is presented to us, it is little wonder that our attention is fleeting.

There is an odd logic at work here. Since, as a math fact, "5+3=__" affords only the briefest consideration, what we begin to witness is the attempt to attain integration, not simply through the *accumulation of thin co-present surfaces*, but through the *acceleration of such accumulation*. One need think only of the typical tempo of early elementary school classrooms. What appears on the surface as vigor and enthusiasm is also readable as a type of hysteria and panic. Given that "5+3=__" is understood to be an isolated curricular fragment (i.e., it is "un-whole"), there is no time to deepen it and dwell on it, to slow it down and open it up, because there is simply so much else to get done and so little time. As Wendell Berry suggests, for this way of being in the world of the classroom, "time is always running out" (1983, p. 76). As such, we can witness in so many classrooms (and, in fact, in so much of contemporary life) an ever-accelerating "onslaught" (Arendt, 1969) of ever-new activities and the odd equation of some sort of fulfillment with becoming caught up in such frenetic consumption. Many teachers and children are thereby condemned to constantly striving to "keep up" and to taking on the *failure* to keep up as a personal/pathological problem involving lack of effort or lack of will. Talk of slowing things down, dwelling over something and deepening our experience of it, begins to sound vaguely quaint and antiquated.

An urban sprawl version of curriculum integration thus

becomes convoluted with both a metaphysical and an eschatological belief. First, it is premised on the metaphysical belief that each curricular fragment (e.g., "5+3=___") is what it is independently of everything else, independently of any sustaining relations. In this view, wholeness cannot be a matter of meditating on how "the whole" of our course might be refracted through *this* fragment or *this*, since it is precisely such refraction that is *denied* by this metaphysical assumption of severance and fragmentation. Second, and following from this metaphysical assumption, an urban sprawl version of curriculum integration suggests that wholeness and integrity is always yet-to-arrive. Education thus gets caught up in a type of eschatological anticipation—"an occult yearning for the future" (Berry, 1986) when integrity and health and wholeness might finally be achieved through the final accumulation of all the "pieces of the picture."

Reflections on a Class in Early Childhood Education: Placing "5+3=8" Back into All Its Relations

In a recent Early Childhood Education "methods" course, we considered the following examples of Grade One children's "math facts" work:

1) 5+3=8
2) 5+3=8
3) 5+3=8

It was proposed that we had found these three samples in the files of three different children who have just entered our classroom. The following questions were posed: What do we now know about these children, about these samples? What do they mean? What do they show? As expected, the answer, for the most part, was "very little." One student ventured that "these children know how to add."

Through a combination of considerations of Jean Piaget's notion of operations (1952), working ourselves with manipulative materials, and, especially, frequent visits to a wonderful Grades One through Four multiage classroom, what slowly became visible underneath the surface-presentation of "these children know how to add" was a roiling nest of multiple operations, multiple voices: "threads interweaving and criss-crossing" (Wittgenstein, 1968, p. 32). Rather than reading each "5+3=8" pathologically, as an isolated *fact*, we slowly became able to read each as a *sign* pointing beyond its isolation to a whole world of implicate relations, a whole "chaos of possibilities" (Hillman, 1987).

One child holds five and counts on. A second counts them all out, showing us not only his own ways of working in mathematics, but showing us also that the child who can hold five is holding not just a "math fact" but a crystallized and stabilized nest of operations that this second child still needs to concretely re-embody and re-enact. Differently put, "5" is itself a doing full of underworlds of relations and connections and threads (for example, the accomplishment and stability of 1 to 1 correspondence and ordinal numerical sequences, the infinite implicate iterations of relations of "4+1," "3+2," "12-7," the square root of 25 and so on) *some of which* this child who holds five understands, some not, but all of which surround and house and make understandable and locatable his work, his efforts, and his experiences. This child's work lives in these implicate relations and is deeply meaningful and sustainable only *within* them (and this in spite of the fact that some of these relations are, from the point of view of the child's own experiences, "beyond him" at this juncture. This is a profound and difficult ecological point—our lives and actions are sustained in part by what is beyond us, beyond what we know, experience, or construct). Another child "just knows the answer" but cannot articulate the operations she performs. Another gets caught up in such articulations and takes on the task of filling out all the permutations of operations embedded in the question at hand, verging, for a moment, near calculus and the formulation of functionally defined sets.

What occurred here was a wonderful but also rather disorienting phenomenon for many student-teachers in this class. They began to see that being stuck in the present tense with the three surface samples and then rushing to accumulate more and more in order to understand "the whole child," (or in order to "cover the whole curriculum") is somehow potentially misguided and unhealthy, for it skitters over the deeply experiential "ecology" of *just this*. "Underneath" the surface of each stubborn particular was an almost overwhelming richness, diversity—hitherto unnoticed communities of relations. But more than this, once opened up, we could begin to see how each stubborn particular—*this* child's work and *this* child's work—becomes reflected and refracted through all the other stubborn particulars, giving all the others shape and place and sense. Differently put, once *this* "5+3=8" becomes *interpretable*, it is no longer an isolated *given* which simply is what it is independently of everything else, like the unread work samples found in the children's files. It becomes "readable" as a multivocal *sign* which portends a whole nest of sustaining relations that are always already wholly at work and without which this stubborn particular would not be what it is. Each stubborn particular thus becomes placed within a nest of possibilities that houses and sustains it. It becomes, in this deeply ecological sense, *whole*, through the slow, meticulous, disciplined working out of its relations.

Here we have a wonderful inversion of the metaphysical assumption of the urban sprawl version of curriculum integration. Each curricular fragment is what it is only *in relation* to the "whole," a whole now readable *in* and *through* the stubborn particulars of our lives.

It is important to add that this does not mean that every child should be relentlessly inundated with relations, possibilities, and articulations at every turn. This would simply turn our interpretive efforts into another version of urban sprawl which acts irrespective of where we are and what particular relations are at work "*here* and *here*." This is the profound sense in which the particular is "stubborn": there is no way that we can replace the exquisiteness of *this* particular (child's work, for example). *This* work—*this* "5+3=8"—occurs at an irreplaceable intersection between the world of mathematics, this child's life and breath and attention and experience, the life and relations of the classroom, the hopes and actions and experience of the teacher, the working out of our curriculum and our culture in and through the institutions of schooling, and so on. Differently put, *this* work—the delicacies of this child's slow counting out of "5"—is the "center" of "the whole" of these relations. It is, in its own way, "a sacred place where the whole of the earth comes to rest in relations of deep interdependency."

However (and this cannot be overemphasized, given our culture's tendency to inflate "child-centeredness" to ecologically disastrous proportions) *this* work is, *at the very same time*, peripheral to (yet still housing of) the work of this next child and this. This stubborn paradox is at the core of curriculum integration. On the one hand, "the universe is a fabric of interdependent events in which *none* is the fundamental entity" (Nhat Hahn, 1986, p. 70): curriculum integration is not child-centered or teacher-centered or subject-matter centered, but rather gives up the fundamentalism that underwrites such centration in favor of a *world* of relations. And yet, at the same time:

> The center is [also] everywhere. Each and every thing becomes the center of all things and, in that sense, becomes an absolute center. This is the absolute uniqueness of things, their [stubborn] reality. (Nishitani, 1982, p. 146)

The arrival of each new child in one's class, the arrival of each new piece of work, is thus potentially fecund. Each stubborn particular carries the potential of re-opening and thus re-vitalizing what I have heretofore understood the whole web of delicacies surrounding "5+3=__" to mean. This particular child always counts by twos and seems stuck there in a loop. She disassembles "5" and "3," re-sorts them and adds them two by two by two by two by setting out pairs of small wooden blocks in rows in front of her. This child brings a uniqueness and individuality and irreplaceability to this activity. But her actions are not just that. Her work cannot simply be accumulatively added the "the whole" of what we have heretofore understood "5+3=8" to mean. Rather, because of her work, that whole now "waver[s] and tremble[s]" (Caputo, 1987, p. 7). This fecund new case refracts and cascades through each particular relation that we took to be a given, giving each one a renewed and transformed sense of its relations and place in the whole. Without the arrival of such fecund new cases, and the portend of transformation and renewal that they bring, mathematics would become simply a given set of memorizable (but not especially memorable) facts and rules and would lose its sense of potency and possibility. It would thus lose its integrity as a *living* system.

What we have come upon here is a *discipline* of mathematics which is both open and closed, which has its own patterns and structures and operations, its own arrays of possibilities and potentialities, but which somehow is renewed and made whole by the arrival of the young. If we pay attention to the stubborn particularity of *this* "5+3=8," this arrival need not be caught up in an onslaught of accumulation and acceleration. Our attention to *this* "5+3=8" is slowed and held in place by the wisdoms and disciplines and sustaining relations of this "place" called mathematics. Conceived as a living system (one hopes that this is a warrantable image for our curriculum), mathematics not a fixed *state* (whether already achieved or yet-to-arrive). It is, so to speak, a *way* which must be *taken up* to be a living whole. There is thus a *way* to mathematics. Learning its ways means entering into these ways, making these ways give up their secrets: making these ways *telling* again, making them more generous and open and connected to the lives we are living out. Understanding mathematics thus becomes a type of ecological intimacy which always already contains images of children and the passing on of the wisdoms of the world to the young. Consider this passage as describing the "world of mathematics" and all it sustaining interdependencies:

> Some people are beginning to try to understand where they are, and what it would mean to live carefully and wisely and delicately in a place, in such a way that you can live there adequately and comfortably. Also, your children and grandchildren and generations a thousand years in the future would still be able to live there. That's living in terms of the whole. (Snyder, 1980, p. 86)

Living in terms of the whole requires somehow making the world of mathematics *livable*. As such, it is not enough to simply delve into its indigenous operations and patterns; nor is it enough to simply abandon children to their own devices and, so to speak, let them have their way with mathematics and not teach the difficult lessons of how to pay attention to where they are and what mysteries this place offers.

It is here that we encounter a paradox: making the world of mathematics livable requires going beyond mathematics itself in to the deep, patterned relations of the world which house and sustain the possibility of pursuing mathematics *at all*—patterns of experience and breath and bone and blood. It is in this deeper, fleshier discipline of repeated patterns of operations and structures and doings, mathematics becomes integrated. It becomes whole.

Interpretive Descent and The Mathematicity of the World

The patterned doings of mathematics are themselves not simply isolated facts. Rather, we find in the patterns and structures of mathematics "an anciently perceived like-ness between all creatures and the earth of which they are made" (Berry, 1983, p. 76). Consider how the following passages describe the patterned doings of the human body (pulse, breath), the patterns of our earthly lives (daily and seasonal cycles and rhythms) and the structure of language itself. Consider how these passages show that each of these refracts through all the others:

> The rhythm of a song or a poem rises, no doubt, in reference to the pulse and breath of the poet. But that is too specialized an accounting; it rises also in reference to daily and seasonal—and surely even longer—rhythms in the life of the poet and in the life that surrounds him. The rhythm of a poem resonates with these larger rhythms that surround it; it fills its environment with sympathetic vibrations. Rhyme, which is a function of rhythm, may suggest this sort of resonance; it marks the coincidences of smaller structures with larger ones, as when the day, the month, and the year all end at the same moment. Song, then, is a force opposed to speciality and isolation. It is the testimony of the singer's inescapable relation to the earth, to the human community, and also to tradition. (Berry, 1983, p. 93)

Or, even more mysterious:

> Rhyme leads one no doubt to hear in language a very ancient cosmology. Rhyme is not only an echo from word to word. Arrangement for arrangement, the order of language evokes and mimes a cosmic order. In realizing itself, rhyme is tuned in to [this cosmology]. Rhyme and meter are praise. An indirect theology. (Meschonnic, 1988, p. 93)

Given this, we can see how curriculum integration cannot involve concertedly *adding on* language alongside mathematics or vice versa. Rather, it requires delving into the
mathematicity of language itself—its patterns and structures and rhythms and tones and operations and grammars.
And, once we crack the literalist surface of mathematics
that might render it an isolated discipline, a cascade of
implications ensues: the rhythm of mathematics,
mathematicity of language, the language of music and
rhythm, the music/patterns/rhythms of the world, and, in
the end, the profound mathematicity of the shifts and flutters in a bear's gait as it breaks from a walk into a run.
Differently put, deep in the underworlds of "5+3=__" we
find a strong and sustainable integration of mathematics
into a "bear theme." Or, better, we find the integration of
bears *and* "5+3=__" into a "whole" which embraces them
both, each in their own way, and refracts each through the
other—structure, pattern, rhythm, operation.

This is an exhilarating movement—a type of
meditational and imaginal descent into the crawling underworld of the particularities of our lives. *Every thing*—
even just this red wheelbarrow, or that child's holding five
tight in her fist for fear of losing it—abounds with connections, dependencies, relations. Every thing, every word,
every curricular fragment, is a potential opening in to "the
whole"—"*this* and *this*" (Wallace, 1987, p. 111). More
strongly put, only *through* a deliberate and disciplined attention to the "stubborn particulars" is "the whole" anything more than simply a floating, and, in the end, unsustainable *idea*.

However, there is also a fearsomeness attached to the
realization that the world is not a flat, clean, literal surface
and that our sanity and wholeness/health cannot be had by

skittering across such surfaces, however safe and secure such surfaces might appear at first glance. There is a fearsomeness attached to the realization that the world is *interpretable*, alive with implications and complicities that are always already at work in the intimacies of our everyday experiences, and that we cannot always control and predict what relations we might stumble on in the dark, no matter how well-laid our (lesson) plans might be.

But none of this goes quite far enough. The mathematicity in the gait of a bear as it breaks from a walk into a run is, in the end, a topic which still simply "floats." We could just as easily have mapped out the parabolic curve of its shoulders or counted its toes or graphed its offspring or life span in relation to other animals. The sort of interpretive descent that curriculum integration requires of us is far more fearsome and more experientially immediate than this allows.

In dwelling upon the mathematical changes in the gait of a bear as it moves from a walk to a run, I cannot avoid coming to reflect on my own living involvement in such earthly rhythms, an "anciently perceived likeness" (Berry, 1983, p. 76) that embraces us both and makes the life of each complicit in the other. In walking up this hill and feeling the fluttering mathematical patterns of breath and pulse and steps, I come to better understand this creature and its mathematical being *in place*, housed by flesh and humus, housed by a mysterious immediacy. And, in understanding this creature in this way, I come to understand myself and my own living involvement in the ecological conditions under which this creature lives and in which I live with it, pulling hard at this same air as it curves up the steep valley sides. It is the fleshy mysteries of my own life and my own wholeness and integrity that this bear and its steps pace out. And, it is mathematics—the very mathematics which I now teach my child—which has underwritten technological images of severance, fragmentation, commodification, and mastery that have ravaged this place, this bear's life and thereby mine along with it. To teach mathematics in an integrated way, therefore, requires more than simply dwelling in its indigenous intricacies and patterns. I must help children (and myself) place mathematics back in to the embrace of the earth (in to the embrace of its kin, like the symmetries of these pine branches). Such embrace will help make it more generous and forgiving and livable than it has become in the severities of our curriculum guides and the severities and violences of our unsustainable beliefs in its dominion as a "Father Tongue" (Le Guin, 1987) which silences all others.

It will help make it (and ourselves, and our children, and this bear, which paces out a life beyond our dominion) whole.

Concluding Remarks

> It is impossible to divorce the question of what we do from the question of where we are—or, rather, where we think we are. That no sane creature befouls its own nest is accepted as generally true. What we conceive to be our nest, and where we think it is, are therefore questions of the greatest importance. (Berry, 1986, p. 51)

Just as it is my own wholeness and integrity that this bear and its steps pace out, so too it is my own wholeness and integrity that is foretold in *whatever* actions I do here, with these children in the classroom. In another Grade One classroom, children are completing subtraction equations on a white sheet of paper. When they are done, the rectangles, each with one equation, are cut out, curled up, pasted on Santa's beard and posted for parents to see during the Christmas concert and classroom visits that surround it.

If we meditate for a moment on this activity, there is a sense in which it is, frankly put, insane. This is not to say that some children might not enjoy it. It is it to say that fostering such enjoyment abandons children to a flickering, hallucinatory vision of the earth, of mathematics, of the events surrounding Christmas, that is, in the end, an ecological and spiritual disaster that no amount of acceleration and accumulation can outrun. Such activities suggest that we no longer know where we are. Such activities, too, are disturbingly suggestive of where we might *think* we are.

In this chapter, I have been suggesting that curriculum integration requires a concerted, thoughtful resistance to such skittering hallucinations. To prevent the woozy visions often associated with such matters, curriculum integration and the wholeness it portends must not sidestep a disciplined, mindful attention to the "stubborn particulars of grace." But there is another suggestion here: these examples of math facts on a teddy bear's tummy and Christmas subtraction equations bear witness to a terrible logic that many teachers and children are suffering *on our behalf*. This is one of the agonies of ecological mindfulness: my own life is implicated in these very examples—*"this and this"*—as is my son's. This difficult knowledge, more than anything, is at the heart of curriculum integration and the ecologies of experiential education.

CHAPTER Six

ECOPEDAGOGICAL REFLECTIONS ON CURRICULAR INTEGRATION, SCIENTIFIC LITERACY, AND THE DEEP ECOLOGIES OF SCIENCE EDUCATION

No matter the distinctions we draw, the connections, the dependencies, remain. To damage the earth is to damage your children. (Berry, 1986, p. 13)

Ecopedagogy

THE TERM *ECOPEDAGOGY* is meant to reawaken a sense of the intimate connection between ecological awareness and pedagogy. This connection is not the outcome of a concerted application of the principles and practices of one domain (ecology) to another domain (pedagogy). Such questions of "domains" and "application" between ecology and pedagogy inadvertently assume the separation of these two disciplines and assume as well that somehow the connections between the sustainable generativities of the earth and the generativity represented by children and embraced by pedagogy are somehow ours to make, not make or unmake. As the passage from Berry suggests, such matters are not at our disposal or discretion to connect or disconnect. More pointedly, these matters are not at our disposal to ignore under the guise of "working in another area."

Even in the realm of the science curriculum, ecology is never simply a *topic* that we might cover. Our science curriculum itself, *whatever* its topic, already embodies long-standing images of ourselves, images of the earth and our place and standing in its ways, the need for ecological responsibility, and images of the nature, limits, and necessities of human understanding. Science is a vision of our "course." But this "our" must itself be unpacked, for the science curriculum embodies as well a particular Eurocentric history in which particular spiritual and epistemological forces are at work that have profound and convoluted ecological consequences (as the current state of our earth attests, suffering as it is under this history; see Berman, 1983; Bordo, 1988; Spangler & Thompson, 1991; Jardine, 1990a, 1992a).

These particular spiritual and epistemological assumptions include images of Rationality as a form of dominion over things, parallel images of colonialism (that is, the right of European forms of life, under the rule of Reason, to dominate and subjugate others) and the heretofore unbridled belief that the earth is ours to do with as we please.

We can think, for example, of the nebulous origins of modern science in the work of Descartes and how, through the process of a methodical doubt of every form of connection or relation we have to our embodied selves and to our earth, Descartes recovered a clear and distinct and indubitable "I think." This "I think" was thought to be separate from the earth and severed from any sense of earthly embodiment, obligation, necessity, or ecological consequence. The clarity and distinctness of this separate "I," coupled as it was with the indubitabilities of mathematics and logic, became the foundation from which the methods of the then-emerging sciences took their cue. Mathematics and logic became, so to speak, the portals through which this self-secure and separate "I" could get back in touch with the earth while still holding fast to the clarity and distinctness it had won through the process of methodical doubt. In this way, under the Enlightenment legacy, Rationality (conceived after logic and mathematics) became, to use Piaget's (1952, p. 19) term, "self-regulating." Reason became the arbiter of all things, able now, in its puffy self-assurance, to demand that the earth must henceforth live up to the clarity and distinctness requisite of mathematization (which itself lives up to the clarity and distinctness of the self-present, indubitable "I think").

Differently put, under the Enlightenment legacy, only to the extent that the earth can be mathematized can the claims we make about it be said to be true.

Another assumption that underlies this Eurocentric history of the science curriculum is far older than Descartes, but it dovetails with his work in powerful ways. Descartes inherited from Thomas Aquinas, and, before that, Aristotle, a belief in substance as an underlying principle of the truth of things: "A substance is that which requires nothing except itself in order to exist" (Descartes 1955, 255). To understand some earthly phenomenon, then, we must begin by severing its intimate and often mysterious and multiple connections not only with ourselves (as Descartes' methodical doubt was wont to accomplish) but also with all other things. A thing is most truly itself when it stands by itself; differently put, because "in truth" a thing needs nothing except itself to exist, to understand it in truth is to understand it separately from all other things. The methods of mathematization that inform the science curriculum—and that are consonant with this notion of separate substances—therefore begin with the assumption that "to understand" means "to sever" and dissect. Thus the methodological isolation of a separate "I" becomes coupled with the belief that to understand is to disintegrate, to divide, to separate, to disconnect.

Thus begins a long cascade of ecological consequences that we are still living out. This set of moves cascading down from the Enlightenment underlies the current unquestioned belief that, to understand ourselves or our earth, we must revert automatically to experimental studies that have mathematics at their core. We automatically believe that rich narrative tales, for example, those of Native North Americans about how fish came to the river, are little more than metaphorical fictions that do not bespeak the truth of such matters. If things are what they are independently of everything else (the scholastic notion of "substance"), the discourse appropriate to this separate, singular, self-identical entity is a discourse that is itself full of the language of self-identity and the singularity of definition, and free of contradiction, ambiguity, mystery, and interdependencies of sense and significance:

> Descartes' emphasis on clear and distinct ideas served to canonize the Aristotelian principles of non-contradiction [A=A]. Since the Cartesian paradigm recognizes no self-contradiction in logic, and since logic,

according to Descartes, is the way nature behaves, the
paradigm allows for no self-contradiction in nature.
(Berman, 1983, p. 23)

The deep-seated belief in what could be called the
univocity of reality (a way of reframing the notion of substances as being what they are independently of everything
else: following the Aristotelian principle of noncontradic-
tion, a substance is what it is, A=A) requires that speech
about such univocal entities must itself be univocal. Any
talk of the earth that carries with it ambiguity, narrativity,
metaphor, multiplicity, contradiction, or the like cannot be
considered *true* because the truth of things (their "substance") is assumed at the outset to be itself clear and distinct. Tales of how fish came to the river—tales that implicitly and necessarily contain a deep mystery and
multivocality, tales that are told differently to each child,
to each generation because their living sense depends on a
nest of intimate, power-laden relations, tales that bespeak
an obligation, a fleshy attachment of fleshy consequence—
all this, under the Enlightenment legacy, is banished from
the realm of that which could be considered "true."

Not only are such tales cut off from what is considered
to be "knowledge," but also what is thus severed is culturally and educationally and spiritually degraded into a form
of "knowledge" that cannot live up to the arbitrations of
Reason. Such tales become ghettoized in ways that parallel the current educational ghettoization of "the humani-
ties" from the "real-world" practicalities and
employabilities of technical and scientific courses in school.
Worse yet—and our Eurocentric history demonstrates this
again and again—the self-assurance that Eurocentric Reason has provided us allows us (in fact, morally obligates

us) to use whatever means necessary to replace these indigenous forms of "knowledge" with the rule of Reason.
And this replacement is done with the most beneficent of
pedagogical motives: "for their own good" (Miller, 1989).
In effect, our implicit Enlightenment images of language,
understanding, and reasonability become a new form of
(albeit unintended) colonialism because they simply reproduce the conditions for replacing multivocity and diversity of living systems with a single voice. This is what
Habermas (1973) named the monological character of scientific discourse.

In these hidden ways (and these few comments provide
the merest hints), education (and the science curriculum
in particular) contains profound ecological consequences
and choices that have *already been made* and are *always
already at work* prior to "ecology" becoming a special topic
of the sciences. And it is clear that this Enlightenment
legacy that informs science and the science curriculum
does not inform them alone: education in general and our
culture as a whole are caught in the sway of this age-old
logic of dismemberment and disintegration. We see the
separation and isolation of the disciplines, we see the mathematization of accountability and of judgment of what is
good in students' work, we see the reduction of
student-teaching to performance checklists that count the
frequency of eye-contact episodes instead of addressing
whether our contacts with children are genuine and real,
and we see the unquestioned cultural predominance of
schooling in scientific and technical forms of knowledge
as keys to living well.

However, we can also see all around us signs of the
struggle to replace this *egologic* (that is, this logic that rests
on the self-certainty of the "I am") with a more delicate

ecologic that places human life back into the sustaining relations and interdependencies (*ecos*) that house and protect and nurture it. This ecologic is one that is necessarily tolerant of ambiguity and diversity and multiplicity. It is one that does not begin with the assumption of clear and distinct and univocally separable substances, but with the assumption of a deep and mysterious interdependency and "wholeness" that embraces and sustains our efforts to understand. Although this is not the context in which to detail this, we can simply say this: ecology is teaching us that a substance (the true character of a particular entity) is not "that which requires nothing except itself in order to exist." Rather, a "substance"—for example, this pine tree outside my window—requires *everything else* to exist. It therefore "exists" in relations of mutuality and interdependence that resist the attempt to "straighten things out" through severance and dissection. We do not deeply understand this pine tree simply through dissecting its oxygen-producing capabilities and the correlative oxygen requirements of the human circulatory system. We deeply understand it by living with this tree in such a way that our dependency on it (the one that science might help us "objectively demonstrate") can go on in a wholesome, sustainable way. Ecologically, we deeply know about this interdependency only to the extent that our knowing makes unthinkable acts that might contravene it.

The ecopedagogical insanity we face is that, under the form of knowledge of our Enlightenment legacy, we can fully and meticulously "understand" our deep dependency on the environment through an objective exploration of oxygen production and consumption, and at the same time act in such a way that such objective knowledge-of-dependency does not at all inform how we live and breathe. This peculiar, low-level insanity is the most profound consequence of the Cartesian severance, and our schools are full of its consequence: schooling has become, in many quarters, irrelevant to the lives we are actually living. More profoundly, the world into which we are often schooling children and that world's vision of "the lives we are actually living" have become wound up in ecological insanities and impossibilities:

> What we call the modern world is not necessarily and not often the real world, and there is no virtue in being up-to-date in it. It is a false world, based upon economies and values and desires that are fantastic, a world in which millions of people have lost any idea of the materials, the disciplines, the restraints, and the work necessary to support human life, and have thus become dangerous to their own lives and to the possibility of life. (Berry, 1983, p. 13)

The allure of this "modern world" comes, in part, from the self-satisfying belief that we are separate, un-earthly entities who can act with "freedom," "independence," and "empowerment" and without any deep or considered sense of where we are and what are the binding relations that hold us in place sustain our ability to act at all.

But again, as Berry (1986, p. 51) suggests, this loss of a deep sense of dependency and relatedness and place has its consequences:

> It is impossible to divorce the question of what we do from the question of where we are, rather, where we think we are. That no sane creature befouls its own nest is accepted as generally true. What we conceive to be our nest, and where we think it is, are therefore questions of the greatest importance.

The ability to sever our understanding and our living is not just an ecological but an ecopedagogical insanity because it has at its heart consequences for the ability of life to go on, and, in such consequences, children, and what we shall tell them of our lives, what we shall show them through our living, are already present. Ecopedagogy is therefore not simply the application of ecological issues to pedagogy or making ecology a special topic in our schools. Nor is it simply the random examination of philosophical theories or historical trends or happenstances—as if the examples cited above could remain at the level of mere babble and quarrel and were not matters of bone and breath and blood that affect how we carry ourselves on the earth. Ecopedagogy is the interpretive unearthing of the ecological entrails implicit *in our pedagogy* itself and the working out of a pedagogy that is more ecologically generous and sustainable, deeply linked to the earth's "limits of necessity and mystery" (Berry 1983,13). It begins with an embodied sense of living urgency and a belief that, beneath the clear and distinct and calm surfaces of our curriculum guides and the often lifeless curriculum models and visionary inventions of educational theory and practice, must beat a real, fleshy heart.

This ambiguous, fleshy kinship between ecology and pedagogy can be simply framed, although its implications pose enormous questions to our lives as pedagogues and to the telling tales that underlie our practices:

♦ To the extent that ecology considers the conditions under which life can go on (Smith, 1988), it is always already intimately pedagogic at its heart.

♦ To the extent that the task of pedagogy is to usher children into those understandings of the earth's ways required for life to go on in a full, healthy, wholesome, and sustainable way, it is already intimately ecological at its heart.

Finally, at the heart of the notion of ecopedagogy hides a traumatic twist already hinted at. It is possible to work with full confidence and fully gracious intent in the area of pedagogy and yet betray an unintended ecological insanity. We can speak with grand aspirations of our hopes for our children or of our faith in a particular vision of the science curriculum while remaining unaware of how those very aspirations, in their ecological assumptions and consequence, might work against the actual breath required to utter them. The ecopedagogical task of developing a more ecologically sane pedagogy is becoming more and more urgent because, even with all our detailed objective knowledge and our command and control over the methods of logic and mathematics, we can do the impossible: we can unintentionally live in a way that works against the real, earthly conditions under which the pedagogy to which we aspire is actually possible.

Curricular Integration
and the Deep Ecologies of Science Education

Much is being made these days of the integration of curriculum and the articulation of a sense of continuity and connection in education over the early grades. This movement is not restricted to the sphere of education but is part of a wider and deeper shift in our understanding of ourselves and our tasks as educators. We are witnessing, on an array of fronts, questions of integrity/integration and wholeness and continuity. These phenomena have convoluted etymological roots that hint at the depth and difficulty we confront in addressing "curricular integration":

> The concept of health is rooted in the concept of wholeness. To be healthy is to be whole. The word health belongs to a family of words: heal, whole, wholesome, hale, hallow, holy. (Berry, 1983, p. 103)

Curriculum integration thus is not an isolated phenomenon that falls under the purview of education alone. It is a sign of far deeper and more intimate shifts in our questioning of the wholeness/integrity of our "course."

Consider the following passage (Snyder, 1980, p. 86) and note how it bristles with pedagogical images interlaced with ecological ones:

> Some people are beginning to try to understand where they are, and what it would mean to live carefully and wisely, delicately in a place, in such a way that you can live there adequately and comfortably. Also, your children and grandchildren and generations a thousand years in the future will still be able to live there. That's thinking in terms of the whole fabric of living and life.

These words contain images of curricular knowing, images of our course, of children, of our responsibilities to a place, and of the nature and limits and necessities of human understanding. Following this, we could consider, for example, how we might live in this "place" of science and science curriculum in a way that leads to a sense of conviviality and harmony, a sense of wholeness and integration with the whole fabric of living and life. How might we consider the "deep ecologies" (Devall & Sessions, 1985) of science education? That is, how might we place science education back into the living relations that sustain and nurture it, that allow it to lead to wholeness and integrity, conviviality and harmony?

We might appear, at this point, to be at a peculiar impasse. I have written at great length regarding how our Enlightenment legacy orients, not to conviviality and harmony, but to a logic of severance and disintegration, and how this logic is working itself out in our educational theories and practices. Ecology is telling us that this logic will no longer do. Does this mean that science itself will no longer do?

Clearly, this implied rejection of modern science and technology will not suffice. It will not do for ecology to suggest some sort of reversion to prescientific ways of being. This simply romanticizes ecological mindfulness and thus repeats a sense of otherworldly fancifulness that diverts our attention from the issues at hand. What ecology does make visible, however, are the ways in which, under our Enlightenment legacy, we have allowed science, scientific rationality, and its technological consequences to become unquestioningly paradigmatic and equally unquestioningly self-regulating in our understanding of ourselves and our world. Ecology would not suggest that science or science education is the problem. Rather, the distention, distortion, and inflation of this form of knowing are at issue. Science and science education have, in a telling way, lost their sense of place and therefore lost sight of any sense of mutuality and conviviality that might make them livable.

Berry (1983) makes a telling point in this regard that puts into perspective our unbridled enamorment with scientific knowledge and the debasement and decline of the deep integrity of science into the hands of bureaucratic "tyrannese":

> Our knowledge of the world instructs us first of all that the world is greater than our knowledge of it. To those who rejoice in abundance and intricacy, this is a source of joy. To those would-be solvers of "the human problem" who hope for knowledge equal to (capable of controlling) the world, it is a source of unremitting defeat and bewilderment. The evidence is overwhelming that knowledge does not solve "the human problem." Indeed, the evidence overwhelmingly suggests...that knowledge is the problem. Having the ability and desire to know, how and what should we learn? And, having learned, how and for what should we use what we know?

Berry (pp. 65-6) follows this with a stunning statement often lost in educational circles:

> One thing we do know is that better solutions than ours have at times been made by people with much less information than we have. We know, too, from the study of agriculture, that the same information, tools, and techniques that in one farmer's hands will ruin land, in another's will save and improve it. This is not a recommendation of ignorance. To know nothing is, after all, no more possible than to know enough. I am only proposing that knowledge, like everything else, has its place, and that we need urgently now to put it in its place.

Science (and, with it, the science curriculum) is reaching a strange limit: it is finding that other voices, other "ways" of understanding and articulating our place on the

earth are asserting themselves, not only as viable alternatives to science but also as alternatives that have a
long-standing sense of proven possibility, practicality, and
worth. What is occurring at this turn in our century is a
breakdown of the unwarranted belief that anyone can speak
on behalf of us all. What is breaking down is the unwarranted belief that a single form of knowing will satisfy us in
the rich diversities of our living. But more than this is occurring. What is also breaking down is the belief that we
can deeply understand any single form of knowing (for example, the type of knowing and corpus of knowledge indigenous to science) in isolation from the rich diversity of
alternatives to it. Curriculum integration is aimed at re-
vealing multiple meanings that undergird a rich, sustainable, living understanding. It does not work against the
deep integrities of any one discipline. (And I suggest this
even though we have all witnessed, in the early grades,
how integration is so often accomplished at the expense of
the integrity of each discipline, a type of "surface integration" that flattens the integrity and difficulty of each in
favor of a woozy, new-agey, infantalizing vision of "the
whole.") An ecologically sound sense of curriculum integration portrays each discipline in its strength by bringing
it into relation with its alternatives. Without a rich understanding of how we might understand this ecological story
through tales and poetry, through history, or through the
dances of language and art—without a rich understanding
of all these, a scientific understanding loses its sense of
place, its sense of proportion; we lose the ability to see the
exquisiteness and irreplaceability of a scientific account
of some phenomenon. Without all its relations, it becomes
potentially disproportionate, potentially monstrous.
     Without the full, diverse, rich array of alternative voices,

the specific character of science as a particular way of knowing becomes lost. What is lost, then, is precisely an integral sense of what difference a scientific understanding might make because it is never brought into proximity with that which is other than it (except, very often, in ways that degrade this "other" at the outset: a poetic tale about this ecological story is not in fact true and therefore cannot help keep a scientific explication of this ecological story in place).

This is the deepest loss of the Enlightenment legacy. Because of the unbridled ascendancy of scientific knowledge and its reckless replacement of the diverse alternatives to it, we became no longer able to raise the question of whether a scientific understanding, in some particular circumstance, might be *best*.

The logic of disintegration and severance at the heart of the science curriculum might serve well its indigenous methodological needs, and ecopedagogical considerations need not enter into this fray with romantic suggestions that science should be otherwise. However, that indigenous logic cannot help us decide whether, in this case or that, science might be the best way to proceed. *This* knowledge of what might be best requires a broadly based, integrated understanding of the multiplicities of knowing in the midst of which and *only* in the midst of which, science might be decisively understood. It requires a sense of the community (ethos) and the world (ecos) that surrounds and houses science and keeps it in place.

Scientific Literacy

To be able to raise such ecopedagogical questions about

science and the science curriculum, we must find ways to break the spell of our enamorment with its methods and corpus of knowledge. This will help us begin to put science back into place, to locate it as a kind of knowing that has a character like and unlike other ways of being in the world. We must unearth an old wisdom: that science, as a form of meticulous attention to the world, cannot decide, in and of itself, if its form of attention is best or most appropriate to the lives we are living or the task that we face because, considered in and of itself, it does not appear in any rich horizon of consideration that might give us this sense of proportion. An age-old wisdom is that no way of proceeding is always and everywhere the best way to proceed.

Out of relation to all the other disciplines and ways of thought and action, questions of the place and appropriateness of *this* discipline simply disappear—we lose a sense of the community (ethos) and the world (ecos) that would help us make an ethically and ecologically sane decision. Thus, pursuing some ecologically viable vision of an "integrated curriculum" is not just a newfangled way of organizing classroom activities and the like. It bespeaks an old wisdom having to do with a sense of place and with the deep knowledge that comes from such a sense. It has to do, therefore, not simply with how understanding operates *in* science but with the understandability *of* science as a human enterprise among others.

I suggest that this ecopedagogical sense of integrated understandability has consequences for the notion of "scientific literacy." Let me put this forcefully: becoming thoroughly versed in the methods and the corpus of scientific knowledge, if this is pursued out of relation to a broader, more integrated sense of the rich array of human life, is, in fact, a form of *institutionalized illiteracy.* "Scientific literacy" in a more ecologically considerate sense would necessitate that we become able to "read" the methods and corpus of the science curriculum *in relation to* the similarities and differences that house it, that give it its particular, powerful place. Only in integrated relation to the whole of human life can we become literate about any part of that life. Only in relation to the whole of human live can we become literate about science.

I therefore suggest that "curriculum integration" is not simply a good idea. It is a condition of an ecopedagogically sane understanding of each discipline that makes up our course. Despite our Enlightenment legacy, we cannot understand science out of relation to all other things. To be what it is, it requires *everything else* to exist in a generous, sustainable way.

Seven
"EVEN THERE, THE GODS THEMSELVES ARE PRESENT"

I

ERMENEUTICS IS NOT FOUNDED upon the separation of researchers from the earthly life they live or the lives that are the topics of their research. Such a sense of separation and isolation and breakdown is often demanded, in all places, of research into the lives we live with our children: educational research.

A great deal of educational research focuses upon methodological issues of how researchers can properly separate themselves from what they are studying. Once the object of their study becomes precisely this, an object that stands over and against the researcher, separate, apart, with all threads of kinship and obligation now severed, the question then is this: How might we safely make warrantable, generalizable, anonymous, methodologically reproducible contact with this object, contact that is pure and unadulterated, contact that is now celibate, uncontaminated by the flesh? This focus on methodology in educational research—which, of course, must *pretend* that we are strangers to our children, and which must also hand our children back to us anonymously, generalizably, faceless, unrecognizable—collapses into a paradoxical desire to *maintain such separation* (i.e., maintain "objectivity") while at the same time *overcoming such separation* (i.e., being able in the end to make claims *about* those things *as* separate from the researcher).

Thus arise bizarrely convoluted ethical and epistemological and ontological quandaries. Ecological nightmares. Dead ends, where "breakdown" becomes the central image of "the basics" of education and educational research. And more than this, the touching events of our lives with our children, and the comfort—the common strength or fortitude—we might gain in deeply understanding such events—all this is lost. In the face of such research, and, admittedly, this oddly human desire for fixity and finality and death, I myself begin to break down.

Hermeneutic work requires me to begin elsewhere. I begin, not at some fantasized place of clarity and distinctness and methodological security, but begin, rather, having already begun: in the midst of the roil of everyday events, everyday experience, in the midst of the life I've lived, in the midst of what has become of me after all these years. The goal of hermeneutic work is not to "methodologically contact" that life from a place of purposeful estrangement, a place of methodological decontamination (again, here, "method" appears as the cause and cure of separateness, the cause and cure of contact). Hermeneutics maintains that such ideas of "contact" and "separateness" always come too late. The ordinary events of our lives are always and already full of relations, full of the whole complex of human inheritance, full of voices and spooks and spirits and desires and tongues, and full of inheritances far beyond the human voice, rivers and soiledges and the coming of this solstice storm. Small events thus become potentially "fecund," presenting themselves as gates or ways in to the luscious roil beneath the skin of familiarity.

Ecoeroticism. "The spell of the sensuous." (Abram 1996)

So, since hermeneutics does not begin with the presumption of the separation of subject and object, of researcher and topic, it also does not begin with the problem of the proper contact between these two things. A hermeneutic conception of "truth," therefore, cannot be one of a correspondence between the claims of a methodologically estranged subject and the object about which claims are being made.

A "correspondence theory of truth" will simply not do. More strongly put, the correspondence between two things produced of breakdown (a "subject" and the "object" of inquiry), seems closer, ecologically, to Wendell Berry's image (1977) of how two such severed things both bear wounds that memorialize and bear witness to their once-belonging-together.

II

Kai enthautha, "even there," at the stove, in that ordinary place where every thing and every condition, each deed and thought is intimate and commonplace, that is, familiar, "even there," in the sphere of the familiar, einai theous, "the gods themselves are present." (Heidegger, 1947, p. 234).

Let's begin with an ordinary classroom event that will help make visible how a hermeneutic sense of "truth" is something different than this string of sad, ecologically disastrous denials. As we shall see, small events of everyday life and not objects to be methodologically manipulated and controlled. Everyday events can often be moments of invitation to *think* of their rich complicities in this earthly life.

I was engaged in practicum supervision this past semester and happened into a Grade Two classroom. The children were filling in a photocopied worksheet, purportedly dealing with questions of addition and subtraction. Here is an example of the question layout: *There are four horses in the field. Two of them run away. How many horses are left in the field?* Beside each question was a little black-line cartoon (in this cases, of "horses"), a line upon which to put your answer, and, above this line, a plus and a minus sign, one of which you were instructed to circle, to demonstrate the operation you used in solving the question. The children were instructed, as well, to "answer on the line in a number sentence." (I will avoid, at this point, going into the discussion I had with three children about the fascinating difference between a "number sentence" and a "sentence with numbers in it").

One student waved me over to them. She said, "I don't understand this one at all." The question she had trouble with was this: *Joan went to the post office. She mailed five letters and three packages. How many more letters than packages did she mail?*

I squatted down beside the student's desk and put up five fingers on one of my hands and three on the other.

"Ok," I said, moving the appropriate hand slightly forward in each case, "she's got five letters and three packages. She's got more letters..."

The student suddenly grabbed the thumb of my "letters" (five digits extended) hand and bent it down. She then bent down my little "pinky" finger as well, leaving three fingers extended. But then, with a puzzled look, she considered my other (three fingers extended) hand. Carefully, she pulled my thumb and little "pinky" finger up, now leaving five fingers extended where there were three, and three fingers extended where there were five.

"Two!" she said, a bit too loud for the enforced quiet that worksheets inevitably demand.

"Yep, two, you've got it."

The student looked back down at the worksheet's requirements. Suddenly, this: "But, you know, I'm not sure. Did I add or subtract?"

With this child's question, the whole enterprise we'd entered began to "waver and tremble" (Caputo, 1987, p. 7). Even here, in a Grade Two classroom, where every event is already foreclosed, where every activity is commonplace and ordinary and not worthy of much attention, here, the gods themselves can be present.

I'm not precisely sure how to describe what occurred here. I do know that, as soon as she uttered these words, there was a palpable sense that something *mathematically important* had just occurred. This child's question was not an object to be fixated upon in order, for example, to assess her mathematical competencies. Rather, this child's question was an invitation. Now the usual epistemological and ecological dead end that erupts with such a claim is this: Whose judgement is this? Who found this inviting? Who experienced this and who didn't? Aren't you just imposing your beliefs and experiences on this child? Who are you to say? Are you just trying to be the mathematics expert who silences others? Oddly enough (but clearly endemic to educational discourses) none of these questions is ever directed towards exploring, unfolding, making some sort of case about and on behalf of *what occurred*, on behalf of *what might be manifest* (about mathematics, about mathematics education, about schools, about worksheets, our images of what children are capable of) in this child's question. Rather, all of these questions presume *at the outset* that we live in separate experiential worlds and that *what occurred* can be broken down into "her experience of what occurred," "my experience of what occurred" and now, reader, "your experience of what occurred." Once thus epistemologically paralyzed—one might even say epistemologically paranoid and timid and withdrawn and depressed—we all withdraw from the world in which we might have met, in which we might have had a conversation over the wonders of mathematical operations and their character and their demands upon us, a world in which others might have read my experience back to me differently than I could have read it to myself, thus saving me from the pretense of my own experience, placing me back in the embrace of a world of relations. Breakdown, again.

Here is the pretense of hermeneutics. In her movement of my fingers, in her insistence at making the five three and making the three five, she, most probably "beyond her wanting and doing" (Gadamer, 1989, p. xxviii), was toying with the belonging-together of addition and subtraction, ideas of the reversibility of operations, of the inverse nature of some operations, and of how, in a mathematically fundamental way, one cannot understand addition without at once understanding its intimate relations to subtraction. This, however, is not an objective property of the original event which, if you stared at it long enough could be found to be just "lying there." Rather, this is an instance of interpretation, that is, trying to accept the claim this event made upon me, accepting the mathematical invitation that this question offered, trying to work it out, open it up, *understand* it.

In the rich topographies of mathematical consciousness—and in spite of the fact that the available "worksheet" had no clear place for this insight, since, of course, this worksheet is premised on breakdown—addition and subtraction belong together and without each other, each one becomes lessened, weakened. Hermeneutics suggests that it is not only possible, but pedagogically necessary to read this student's "I'm not sure…" not as a *problem* that needed to be fixed, or as an occasion to withdraw into epistemological timidity, but rather, as an invitation into a place of deeply mathematical venture, deeply mathematical liveliness. Differently put, hermeneutics resists "subjectivizing/objectivizing" breakdown. It moves towards how *what occurs* might be true of this place in which we've found ourselves, how this "I'm not sure…" might thus help us open up and understand mathematics more generously than this worksheet might have allowed or lead us to expect. But again, here, "true" cannot mean "correspond."

There was this giggly moment of face-to-face pleasure, the feeling that we were on to something interesting, something full of address, something that had claimed our attention, held it and took far better care of it that this worksheet had up until then.

I asked the student to get out a marker and circle this particular question, and we talked, hushed, about how *this was a really good question*. "The others are too easy. You just have to *do* them" she whispered, some secret knowledge that perhaps we'd better not let out.

Except we did. We took the encircled worksheet up to the teacher to show her what we had found and she said, "Yes, I see, this is badly worded. I'd better remove it next time." And so, what was initially a question that opened up a rich, delicious territory to be explored, suddenly became a problem to be fixed. The student's question was thus read as a sign of breakdown needing repair, not a sign of openness and invitation needing to be taken up.

IV

There are three entwined senses in which hermeneutics draws on Martin Heidegger's pre-Socratic nightdreams of *Alethia* for its understanding of the "truth" of hermeneutics. In these senses is something of this incident cited above.

Alethia means to open up what was previously shut, to show what was previously concealed. It was precisely this sense of "something opening up" that that student's question provoked. And, moreover, it was precisely a sense of "closedness" that that origin worksheet contained. What was on that worksheet might appear to be *questions*, but, in fact, since the answers are already at hand (and, make no mistake, our children *know this*), they are only problems that, once fixed, fall from memory and experience.

To understand this classroom event as true is to greet it as an opening into a rich field of relations and memories and ancestries and conversations and contestations that were heretofore covered up, concealed. It is, in this very sense, to take up the rich field of mathematics as a *living discipline*. Thus a second sense.

Alethia means to liven up, to enliven, to see the life in what was previously deadened (lethal), lifeless, boring, obvious. This is the most phenomenological of the characteristics of *Alethia*: it is linked to the adrenaline rush of insight, the giddy breath of generativity and newness ("the new, the different, the true" [Gadamer, 1977, p. 44]) and liveliness, the weird feel that something has *happened.* Opening is a movement, an animation, a coming across in which something seems to turn around and face me and demand, claim, address in a voice that is not my own. This, of course, is precisely the sort of "contamination" that many research modes would condemn as "subjective." But if we venture out into *what is being asked of us mathematically in this child's question*, the topic is no longer "me" or "just this child" as "knowing subjects," but the *place into which we've ventured*, a place which has its own ways.

Lethe was the river one crossed into the underworld, and such crossing involved forgetting what one had undergone or experienced. *Alethia* thus means remembering what was forgotten, recovering what has been lost. We need not configure this in the Platonic sense of remembering a past unearthly life. What is forgotten are the howling ancestries *right there in front of us.* Forgetting is *right there in the work sheet*, which is *produced of* forgetting as much as it *produces* forgetting in the children who simply "do" it. After all, on this black-line surface, what, pray tell, is worth remembering about this worksheet?

Unless, of course, something *happens* that calls us to account: "Did I add or subtract?" Even there, the gods themselves are present if we have the ears.

Eight

REFLECTIONS ON EDUCATION, HERMENEUTICS, AND AMBIGUITY:

Hermeneutics as a Restoring of Life to Its Original Difficulty

E DUCATION IS CONCERNED with the "bringing forth" (*educare*) of human life. It is thus essentially a "generative" discipline, concerned with the emergence of new life in our midst, and what it is we might hope for this new life, what it is we might wish to engender. Ideally, each new child embodies the possibility that things can become other than what they have already become. What could be called a "conservative" reading of this ideal would be one that finds this ideal precisely the *problem* of education: How are we to educe new life in a way that conserves what already is? The opposite extreme is one that finds this ideal to be precisely the *hope* of education: How are we to educe the new? Underlying both of these readings is a more fundamental question: How are we to respond to new life in our midst in such a way that life together can go on, in a way that does not foreclose on the future (Smith, 1988)?

Hermeneutics, "radically" interpreted, is concerned with precisely this issue. It distinguishes itself from other forms of inquiry by its essentially educational nature. That

115

is to say, hermeneutic inquiry has as its goal to educe understanding, to bring forth the presuppositions in which we already live. Its task, therefore, is not to methodically achieve a relationship to some matter and to secure understanding in such a method. Rather, its task is to recollect the contours and textures of the life we are already living, a life that is not secured by the methods we can wield to render such a life our object. The title of Hans-Georg Gadamer's seminal text, *Truth and Method* (1989), is thus essentially ironic: Truth, hermeneutically conceived, has little to do with method. "The hermeneutic phenomenon is basically not a problem of method at all." (p. xi)

Methodical, technically based approaches to inquiry in education offer themselves as essentially *informative*. They are designed to pass on information that is already understood, *given* a certain method or research design and a specific history of inquiry. In such approaches, understanding begins and ends with method and operates in service to such a method. Understanding is thus educationally neutered: it is not designed to educe the possibility of understanding, but *assumes* such a possibility of its ground. This is why Heidegger (1973) maintained that we have come upon an age where the *matters* of inquiry have become matters of method. If we play the original meaning of the word "data," what is most fundamentally granted or given in inquiry is not *the matters themselves*, but rather the *method* whereby what is given is rendered objectively presentable. Such inquiries thereby speak on behalf of themselves and their own methodological self-security. It is to method that such inquires are obedient; it is method that they most fundamentally heed (*ab audire*, to listen, to attend, the roots of the term "obedience").

In the area of education, technical images of inquiry

have come to hold sway, and we have become inundated with research that is aimed at pinning down the life of the developing child in such a way that, in the end, nothing more will need to be said.

> Ideally, research orients to the first articulation of what it means to be a child or an adult, about which nothing more needs to be said, about which no further specification is needed or possible, in relation to which every variable has been controlled such that, in the end, research would dispel the need or the possibility of saying more. Being a child or being an adult would, ideally, become exhausted issues, in need of no further consideration. The impetus of such research seems to be the as-yet-unfixed variable, the discovery of which warrants further research. The goal of such research seems to be silence—the end of the need to address such issues. (Misgeld & Jardine, 1989, p. 270)

In the face of such a prospect—the hoped-for end of the Word—I would like to offer an analogy.

This analogy responds to Caputo's (1987) provocative formulation of hermeneutics as entailing a "restoring of life to its original difficulty" (p. 1). Technical-scientific discourse offers itself up as a *remedy* to the difficulties of life. The analogy developed below implicitly raises the question as to whether technical-scientific discourse, rather than simply being a remedy to life's difficulties, has rather come to recast the nature of life's difficulties into precisely the sort of thing for which a technical solution is appropriate; that is, life's difficulties are technical problems requiring a "technical fix." The hermeneutic critique of technical-scientific images of inquiry and discourse is not an attempt to say that such approaches should proceed oth-

erwise. As Gadamer (1977) maintains, "such pronounce-
ments have always had something comical about them"
since such approaches "will continue along [their] own path
with an inner necessity beyond [their] control, and...will
produce more and more breathtaking *knowledge* and controlling power. It can be no other way" (p. 10). Rather,
hermeneutics wants to recover the original difficulties of
life, difficulties that are concealed in technical-scientific
reconstructions, concealed in the attempt to render human
life objectively presentable. "Original" in the usage does
not mean a longing for some unspecifiable past "before"
technology (a sort of nostalgia) or longing for one's own
past, one's childhood (echoing in some forms of phenomenological pedagogy), but it is nevertheless a longing. It is
a longing for fundamental answers to questions of how life
together can go on in such a way that new life is possible in
our midst (Smith, 1988a).

The problem with technical-scientific discourse is not
some indigenous evil or surreptitious intent; rather it is
found in the way in which such discourse has come to per-
vade the possibility of raising questions about our lives
and the lives of children. The language it offers is *already
foreclosed* (or, at least, it longs for such foreclosure). It longs
for the last word; it longs for a world in which the Word no
longer lives, a world in which the droning silence of objective presentability finally holds sway over human life. The
difficult nature of human life will be solved. We will finally
have the curriculum "right" once and for all. We will have
turned children inside-out and searched out every nook
and cranny. Nothing more will need to be said. Obviously,
no educational theorist or practitioner would actually claim
to want this. But the hesitancy to make such a claim occurs
in the same breath that we hear about "having solved just

one piece of the puzzle, just one part of the picture. Further research always needs to be done." Such talk, even in its admirable hesitancy, already operates with an implicit image of the life of the developing child as an objective picture with specifiable component parts. Our exact specifications may be incorrect and further specification is always possible, but such openness does not disrupt the fundamental belief that human life *is* an objective picture that, however complex, is objectively "there" (Jardine, 1988) to be rendered presentable, piece by relentless piece (Heidegger, 1977). As an "object" of technical-scientific discourse, the possibility of the last Word is what makes that discourse possible, howling as it does, even in its hesitancy. It is *here*, perhaps, that the hermeneutic critique sits most squarely. For it is not the actual procedures, methods, concepts, and orientations of technical-scientific discourse that are at issue, but rather the deep *denial of desire* found in that discourse. What hermeneutics unearths— and it is not alone or exclusive in such a project—is the desire for finality, the desire for control, the relentless human lust to render the world a harmless picture for our indifferent and disinterested perusal. This is why the works of Nietzsche are of such interest to those in the hermeneutic tradition. It was Nietzsche's work that rescued the *will to power* from its various objectifications (God, sense data, substance, mathematics, scientific method). It was this cue that disrupted the desire for foundations, for finality—no longer was it easy to simply point with convincing argument to a *fundamentum* without facing up to our lusty fundamentalism and the dogmatism and literalism it entails. Once the difficult play (*lude*) of life is denied or objectified into some dispassionate *fundamentum* (e.g., statistically documentable results that provide the basis for claims about the life of the developing child), inquiry becomes deluded, unable to face its own liveliness, its own life, its own desire.

Hermeneutics does not wish to enter into the fray with an alternate foundation. The returning of life to its original difficulty is a returning of the possibility of the living Word. It is a return to the essential generativity of human life, a sense of life in which there is always something left to say, with all the difficulty, risk, and ambiguity that such generativity entails. Hermeneutic inquiry is thus concerned with the ambiguous nature of life itself. It does not desire to render such ambiguity objectively presentable (as if the ambiguity of life were something to dispel, some "error in the system" that needed correction) but rather to attend to it, to give it a voice. And it does this while recognizing its own embeddedness in the very life of which it is the expression. Its manner of speaking is therefore not "informative," standing outside of the ambiguity of life as a voyeur demanding a good show, demanding presentability. It is, rather, provocative, a prophetic "calling forth," a voice crying out from within the midst of things. It is, therefore, not disinterested, but profoundly interested (*inter esse*—right in the midst of things). But even in such interest, hermeneutics involves a recognition that it is not somnambulatly "at home" in the midst of things. It remains attentive to a certain "uncanniness" (*unheimlichkeit* [Heidegger, 1962)] about our earthly life and wishes to preserve and cultivate (*Bildung* [Gadamer, 1989]) such a sense of alert, animating uncanniness rather than betraying it with metaphysical assurances (Caputo, 1987).

Such an earthly, animate hermeneutics persistently asks anew the question of the place of inquiry; it persistently asks anew after what needs to be said here, in this place, under these stars. Hermeneutics is thus an analogue for human life, conceived not as an objectively renderable picture, but as a "horizon of future...still undecided possibilities" (Gadamer, 1989, p. 101). It involves a recognition that the Word is essentially homeless, with no prescribed method in which it might rest assured of the eventual foreclosure of the question of one's place; it involves a recognition that the Word cannot be pinned down, for when we attempt to do so, the Word will rise again. Such rising anew means that hermeneutics deeply recognizes the place of language, culture, and history in human life and discourse and the propelling ways in which life is irremediably conditioned and contextualized by such phenomena. But it also holds open a place for renewal, for the rebirth of the spirit, for new life. Although hermeneutics may begin here, human life cannot be deeply understood through a thorough historical, linguistic, and cultural interpretation.

In the midst of such potentially dusty and deadened talk, new life interrupts, causing a rupture, a rapture, right in the middle of things. It comes asking for room, hoping for the reenlivenment of human life, needing a place of its own to be born. So again, hermeneutics links up essentially rather than accidentally with education, with the emergence or bringing forth of human life. But let us play out the paradoxical biblical image here and not ignore it. At its birth, the living Word was told that *there was no room*. The living Word had to be born right out in the middle of things, in the embrace of an earth, in the presence of the animals, under the starts, and it was such a birth that made it not only part of what already was but also a heralding of the new, of renewal, the possibility of life.

What, then, is the proper hermeneutic response in education? Is it foreclosure, the denial of room, in order that the Word might live? Perhaps renewal requires our denial, our unwillingness to provide a foundation, a resting spot, room at the inn, room for the soon-to-be-deadly counting of children's heads under Herod's command. But there is the paradox: Perhaps renewal requires our attempts to provide room, provide a foundation that is then denied in the moment of renewal. Perhaps the anti-foundationalism of later hermeneutics and deconstructionism is an attempt to take over renewal for ourselves. Perhaps these are a childish attempt to be the child ourselves and deny childhood to our children. Children become nothing more than interruptions of our own playfulness, needing us to be more sure, more "grounded," more authoritative than we ourselves desire to be. Yet perhaps these are an attempt to understand the precious child in us all, the precious possibility of renewal that constitutes human life. Perhaps it is an attempt to bring forth the living Word in which we *all* dwell, to show that, *even in our authoritativeness as adults*, the Word can live both for us and for children, that child and adult deeply require each other. Perhaps it is an affirmation that none of us need to be deluded, that the precious play of the world is open to all. This paradox will not sit still and resolve itself. It will not finally and definitively touch one axis or another—it is parabolic, a parable that we cannot solve, fix, or ignore. We must simply learn to live with it, and perhaps a properly hermeneutic response is one that savors its ambiguity and is willing to face the difficulty it evokes without withdrawing into either mute, declarative authoritarianism or involving ourselves in the pretense that we are not adults.

> The old unilateral options of gericentrism (appealing to the authority of age, convention, tradition, nostalgia)

and pedocentrism (child-centered pedagogy) only produce monstrous states of siege which are irresponsible to the matters at hand, that is, to the question of how life is mediated through relations between old and young. (Smith, 1988, p. 28)

To bring out the possibility of this provocative return to the living Word that hermeneutics seems to long for—the possibility, one might say, of a true *conversation* between young and old which is not foreclosed by either extreme of reverence for the old *or* titillation with the new—I offer the following analogy.

Animals under various forms of threat—the continuous presence of predators, lack of adequate food, drought, and the like—tend to play less and less. They tend, quite naturally, to revert to those kinds of activities that will aid them in gaining comparative control over their environment, activities that involve little or no risk. They revert, so to speak, to what is tried and true, what is most familiar. Although in times of leisure (paradoxically, the original meaning of *schola*, the root of "school" and "scholar") play may aid in the development of new and more adaptive ways to gain control over the environment, play *itself* does not offer such control, but is rather risk-laden.

As an analogue to this, one could say that a predatory job market and adverse economic conditions have turned education more and more toward the development of "marketable skills" and away from a "liberal" education, which has come to be rather vaguely equated with not knowing how to *do* anything. Education has turned away from the risks of self-transcendence involved in the exploration of many possibilities of understanding, self understanding, and mutual understanding—an exploration in which one is engaged in confronting that which is "other," involving a "moment of loss of self" (Gadamer, 1977, p. 51). It has turned toward the comparative security of self-possession (involved in the accumulation and securing of specific technical skills, intended to give one comparative control over one's place in the world, ways of "having command," not only over the world, but over one's self-understanding [e.g., "I can do this; I have these skills; I have mastered these techniques"]).

I would like to push this analogy one step further, since there is a point at which it fundamentally breaks down.

The increasing specialization of technical knowledge seems to bring with it the perception that one does not really understand the world, oneself, or others without such knowledge. One could witness how, for example, the relentless proliferation of research data on every conceivable feature of the child's life seems to engender the feeling of knowing less and less, of being more and more unable in the face of such proliferation, so that the only way to survive is to diligently attempt to "get on top of things" and try to "pin them down." Because an overwhelming technical knowledge of every conceivable phenomenon is *possible*, this possibility begins to harbor the perception that one is increasingly out of control if one does not *pursue* this possibility. One is increasingly in danger of no longer understanding. Understanding begins to appear possible only to the extent that we have methodically guarded ourselves against the possibility of misunderstanding (Gadamer, 1977). And this perception of being out of control without technical knowledge, of being "left behind," leads precisely to the anxiety that drives us to relentlessly pursue it, since it is precisely technical knowledge that offers us the promise of relative control. Minuscule obedience to the letter of the law seems to ensure salvation, dividing the subdividing human life into the smallest possible manipulable and controllable bits.

In this way, the mere existence of technical knowledge as a possibility creates the need for that possibility by engendering the anxiety for which it sets itself up as the remedy, not the cause. Once human life becomes the object of technical-scientific reconceptualization, the difficulties of that life become understandable only as technical problems requiring technical solutions. Being alive becomes something to *solve*, and finding one's life difficult, ambiguous, or uncertain is a *mistake* to be corrected. In education, once our understanding of being human becomes estranged from the ongoing, interpretive narrative of everyday life (a narrative rife with possibilities, ambiguity, and risk) and is reconstructed into an object ripe for technical manipulation—once the difficulty of human life comes to be seen as a mistake to be corrected—we begin the horrifying task of chasing our own tails with the hope of eventually closing down the risk-laden conversation that such a narrative involves and requires. We begin to be caught up in the exhausting and consumptive pursuit of "mastery" and "excellence" as something that can be achieved solely as a function of individual methodical diligence and effort, and we begin to engender such exhaustion in our children. If such mastery is not achieved, the only recourse we have available is accusation and guilt—one failed to apply oneself, proper instruction was not given, the rules were not made clear. Thus emerges in education the grand reversal where *not* achieving "excellence" must be accounted for against the background of the assumption that everyone can, and should, be excellent. Education becomes a matter of technical specification and manipulation. Nothing is truly *difficult* and *risky*; it is simply effortful, simply a matter of finding out the trick and applying the correct techniques appropriately. The possibility of failure, of error, must be reduced to technical matters that can be fixed by technical means open to everyone and anyone.

With all of this, there is no "play" left in life, not only in the sense of "recreational time" (although even this has become an occasion for vicious and relentless "self-improvement"—a form of "getting ahead") but in the sense that life becomes reduced to its actualities, bereft of the possibility of lateral movement into something new or different, and bereft of any sense that there is *time* for such movement. If we "waste time" dwelling in the ambiguous interplays of life, joining in on the conversation with the texts and textures of human life, we are not "getting ahead" in any securable and specifiable way.

Life becomes haunted by an unnamed grieving for what is lost. It is a grieving for the loss of the ability to actually *face* the troublesome character of life in such a way that life together might itself have a chance (Smith, 1988), in such a way that new life, liveliness, some "movement" might be possible. In the very midst of the breathtaking advance of technology—an advance aimed at *solving* the difficulty of life—private space, the isolation of the Walkman, the computer, television, and video game screens, narcissistic versions of self-improvement (from channeling to Oprah to psychic hotlines) and a peculiar loneliness ensue. Reduced to its actualities, life becomes degenerative, longing for the last word, longing for foreclosure, longing for death. Under the deluge of research reports and more and more detailed objectively presentable specifications of our lives (and the burgeoning rows of books popularly available), one longs for it to be over, to be finally fixed once and for all. Or, in the face of such a deluge, we simply withdraw into self-indulgence, handing over questions of the possibility of life to those "in the know" and understanding ourselves in that withdrawal as peculiarly helpless in the face of such (now technical, now "expert") questions. We become banished to a debilitating and immobilizing form of episodic "individualism" as the last vestige of the Word. ("This is my experience, but then, who is to say who is right? Each of us has our own perspective.")

These have become the grand alternatives: the immobility of technical foreclosure or the immobility of an impotent, only self-annunciating "subjectivity." In both cases, the earth remains unheeded, unhealed; in both cases, our lives become unearthed. The only alternative left to a technological foreclosure and the death of the living Word is the tyranny of subjectivity, which leads us to titillation by bizarre phenomena. It does not help us live *out* our lives together. We simply become attached to televised spectacles that we watch with a sort of immobile, pornographic vicariousness.

In education, we have begun to provoke our children to "keep up," haunted as we are with vague cultural specters of "falling behind" and images of human life as sequentially achieved mastery. Technical-scientific understanding, as a response/cause/correlate of this haunting state begins, as Heidegger (1962) put it, to "take over guidance for Being-in-the-world" (p. 90) by offering itself as that form of understanding that will remedy the anxiety produced by such original estrangement. For example, the experiential method in educational research becomes attractive because of its methodological trustworthiness, providing as it does the feeling that we are actually "getting somewhere" in inquiry. If human life really is something to be mastered, we must place our trust in those methods that offer ways of mastering. In light of this, hermeneutics is often viewed with a deep and understandable suspicion— it seems to be "up to something" that it refuses to specify or make explicit, operating perhaps with some hidden agenda. Whatever it is up to, it seems to be against what "we" take as fundamental. It *claims* to not want to change a letter of the law, but it seems to be persistently negative. In light of a view of human life as something to be mastered, inquiry can be nothing other than a form of fundamentalism, and the difference of hermeneutics can only be a matter of a different foundation, different basic concepts, or a different method of operation. So the question comes up, over and over again, as to what hermeneutic method really is (*even though* it aggravatingly claims that it is not a matter of method). Hermeneutics becomes something impotent and ignorable by being turned into "one more damn thing" (Smith, 1988c), and a rather peevish thing at that, because it refuses to say where it stands. It becomes as impotent and ignorable as children become when we can master and control their difference by being able to fix and locate them on a universal developmental sequence. Hermeneutics, in adamantly refusing to be fixed, becomes nothing more than an undisciplined child (Misgeld & Jardine, 1989).

But if life dwells in an original difficulty, an original ambiguity that cannot be mastered but only lived with well, the pursuit of such mastery can only lead to immobility or exhaustion—it does not lead to *understanding* human life-as-lived in a deep way. Life as something to be mastered seems to deny what we already know about being alive. A hermeneutic notion of understanding is centered on the dispossession of understanding from its methodical, prepared self-security. It returns inquiry in education to the original, serious, and difficult interpretive play in which we live our lives together with children; it returns inquiry to the need and possibility of true conversation.

It is here that the voice of so-called qualitative research in education emerges—in the rich and ambiguous moments of actually living our lives with children, moments in which we cannot proceed with the brazen confidence and clarity of other forms of research—not because of a failure to be precise, but because of the nature of the matters at hand. One begins to attend to the "data" of human life as they are actually given or granted. It is an attentive, and, one might say, appreciative response to that which is given, to this "gift." It is for this reason that Heidegger (1968) rather playfully links up *denken* with *danken*—thinking, inquiry, becomes a form of thanks for what is given:

> The things for which we owe thanks are not things we have from ourselves. They are given to us. We receive many gifts, of many kinds. But the highest and really most lasting gift given to us is always our essential nature, with which we are gifted in such a way that we are what we are only through it. That is why we owe thanks for this endowment, first and unceasingly. (p. 142)

Inquiry in hermeneutics is therefore a form of recollecting what is granted, a way of "gathering" that recognizes how inquiry itself already belongs to the very life for which it gives thanks, that very life which it "thinks." Inquiry so conceived cannot lay out a methodical agenda of pre-given concepts and methods *as if* the epistemic conditions of inquiry take some sort of precedence over the conversation of life itself. A pre-secured method already comes too late in its attempts to render what is already given, prior to such securing. More to the point, such securing is "unthankful" and "unthinking," since it cannot take up this gift as something freely given. Taking up this gift requires a peculiar dispossession of understanding, a "self-transcendence" of which technical-scientific discourse is not capable. Perhaps, then, such approaches should be understood as forms of suspicion and refusal, a wanting to methodically foreclose on the elusive, ambiguous, and tenuous character of what is given, suspiciously seeking motive, cause, or agenda. "The method of modern science is characterized from the start by a refusal: namely, to exclude all that which actually eludes its own methodology and procedures. Precisely in this way it would prove to itself that it is without limits and never wanting for self-justification." (Gadamer, 1977, p. 93) Perhaps this is why Heidegger abrasively says that the sciences do not *think*. In light of this:

> One has to ask oneself whether the dynamic law of human life can be conceived adequately in terms of progress, of a continual advance from the unknown into the known, and whether the course of human culture is actually a linear progression from mythology to enlightenment. One should entertain a completely different notion: whether the movement of human existence does not issue in a relentless inner tension between illumination and concealment. Might it not just be a prejudice of modern times that the notion of progress that is in fact constitutive for the spirit of scientific research should be transferable to the whole of human living and human culture? One has to ask whether progress, as it is at home in the special field of scientific research, is at all consonant with the conditions

of human existence in general. Is the notion of an
ever-mounting and self-perfecting enlightenment finally
ambiguous? (Gadamer, 1983, pp. 104-105)

This notion of an "ever-mounting and self-perfecting
enlightenment" must especially be questioned in the field
of education, for it portends an image of being human in
which generativity—the gift of new life, not only the lives
of children, but also in the sense that our lives, as adults,
can become something other than we might have methodically anticipated—can, in principle, be foreclosed. It portends an image of education as accidental. Even if only
understood in principle, once such enlightenment is
reached, education is no longer needed. Understanding will
not need to be educed; knowledge will simply have to be
reproduced in children, information will simply have to be
handed over. But in this reproduction, in this handing over,
children will have nothing to say, and what we have to say
will have already been said. In fact, their *being* children
will simply be a result of the accident of birth; becoming
an adult will be a technical repairing of the accident of
natality. So this image of enlightenment that underlies
progress reveals itself as little more than an eventual hatred of children, a hatred of the difference they bring, the
difference they make in our lives. If human lives are to
culminate in a foreclosing self-perfection, progress and
mastery must eventually turn on the young who long to
speak, to get in on the conversation, when we as adults
already know that there is nothing left to say.

In the inner tension between illumination and conceal-
ment, the elusive Word can live. Hermeneutically conceived, the task of inquiry is not to dispel this tension, but
to live and speak from within it. It is this tension that pro-

pels the generativity of the Word—that makes education hopeful, that makes it possible. It is its love of this generativity and its longing to open up inquiry to such generativity that makes hermeneutics appear so negative in regard to certain forms of inquiry and discourse. It is this love that undergirds hermeneutics' intolerance of those who would traffic in the business of education as if it were as meaningless, as deadened, as unthankful and unthinking as they propose it to be. It is unimaginable to bring new life into a world in which there is nothing left to say, in which the Word no longer lives. Detached from its original, vibrant difficulty, the original ambiguity, inquiry, and discourse become degenerative, wanting to have the last Word. How can we want this and be educators as well?

CHAPTER Nine

BIRDING LESSONS
AND THE TEACHINGS
OF CICADAS

I WENT BIRDING last summer with some old friends through the Southern Ontario summer forests where I was raised, crackling full of songbirds and head-high ferns and steamy heat. It was, as always, a great relief to return to this place from the clear airs of Alberta where I have lived for eleven years—academic, faculty of education, curriculum courses, practicum supervision in the often stuffy, unearthly confines of some elementary schools.

As with every time I return here, it was once again a surprise to find how familiar it was, and to find how deeply I experience my new home in the foothills of the Rocky Mountains through these deeply buried bodily templates of my raising. It is as if I bear a sort of hidden ecological memory of the sensuous spells (Abram 1996) of the place on earth into which I was born. How things smell, the racket of leaves turning on their stems, how my breath pulls this humid air, how birds' songs combine, the familiar directions of sudden thundery winds, the rising insect drills of cicada tree buzzes that I remember so intimately, so immediately, that when they sound, it feels as if this place itself has remembered what I have forgotten, as if my own memory, my own raising, some of my own life, is stored up in these trees for safe keeping.

Cicadas become archaic storytellers telling me, like all good storytellers, of the life I'd forgotten I'd lived, of deep, fleshy, familial relations that worm their ways out of my belly and breath into these soils, these smells, this air.

And I'm left shocked that they know so much, that they remember so well, and that they can be so perfectly articulate.

I became enamored, during our walk, with listening to my friends' conversations about the different birds that they had been spotting. They spoke of their previous ventures here, of what had been gathered and lost, of moments of surprise and relief, of expectation and frustration. Their conversations were full of a type of discipline, attention, and rich interpretive joy, a pleasure taken in a way of knowing that cultivated and deepened our being just here, in this marsh, up beside these hot, late-afternoon sun-yellowy limestone cliffs.

Updraughts had pulled a hawk high up above our heads. We spotted a red-winged blackbird circling him, pestering, diving.

Sudden blackbird disappearance.

Hawk remained, over a hundred feet overhead, backlit shadowy wing penumbras making it hard to accurately spot.

Where had that blackbird gone?

"There. Coming down the cliff face."

Sudden distinctive complaint around our heads. He had spotted us as worse and more proximate dangers to this marsh than the hawk that'd been chased far enough away for comfort.

My friends' conversations were, in an ecologically important sense, *of a kind* with the abundance of bird songs and flights that surrounded us—careful, measured, like speaking to like, up out of the hot and heady, mosquitoed air. And, standing alongside them there, sometimes silent, certainly unpracticed in this art, involved a type of learning that I had once known but, like cicadas, long-since forgotten.

I had forgotten the pleasure to be had in simply standing in the presence of people who are practiced in what they know and listening, feeling, watching them work.

I had forgotten the learning to be had from standing alongside and imitating, practicing, repeating, refining the bodily gestures of knowing.

I had forgotten how they could show me things, not just *about this place*, but about how you might carry yourself, what might become of you, when you know this place well.

Part of such carrying, such bearing, is to realize how the creatures of this place can become like great teachers (Jardine, 1997) with great patience. Such a realization makes it possible to be at a certain ease with what you know. It is no longer necessary to contain or hoard or become overly consumptive in knowing. One can take confidence and comfort in the fact that this place itself will patiently hold some of the remembrances required: like the cicadas, patiently repeating the calls to attention required to know well of this place and its ways.

So we stood together in the bodily presence of this place. Listening, watching, waiting for knowing to be formed through happenstance arrivals and chance noticings. Seeking out expectant, near-secret places that they knew from having been here before, often evoking slow words of fondness, remembrance, and familiarity—intimate little tales of other times. Repeating to each other, with low and measured tones, what is seen or suspected. Reciting tales from well-thumbed-through books that showed their age and importance. Belly-laughing over the wonderful, silly, sometimes near-perfect verbal descriptions of bird songs: "a liquid gurgling *konk-la-ree* or *o-ka-lay*" for Peterson's (1980, p. 252) version of the red-winged blackbird.

Then settling, slowing, returning, listening and looking anew. Meticulousness: "At the edge, below the canopy of the oak, there, no, left, there, yes!"

These are, in part, great fading arts of taxonomic attention, and the deep childly pleasures to be had in sorting and gathering and collecting (Shepard, 1996). There is something about such gathering that is deeply personal, deeply formative, deeply pedagogical. As I slowly gathered something of this place, it became clear that I was also somehow "gathering myself." And as I gathered something of the compositions of this place, I, too, had to become composed in and by such gathering. And, with the help of cicadas, I did not simply remember this place. Of necessity, I remembered, too, something of what has become of me.

A birding lesson: I *become* someone through what I know.

This little lesson may be the great gift that environmental education can offer to education as a whole. Coming to know, whatever the discipline, whatever the topic or topography, is never just a matter of learning the ways of a place but learning about how to carry oneself in such a way that the ways of this place might show themselves. Education, perhaps, involves the invitation of children into such living ways.

This idea of a knowledge of the "ways" (Berry 1983) of things and the immediacy, patience, repetition, persistence, and intimacy—the "attention and devotion" (Berry 1986, p. 34)—that such knowledge requires, is ecologically, pedagogically, and spiritually vital. It suggests that a knowledge of the ways of red-winged blackbirds is not found nestled in the detailed and careful descriptions of birding guides. Rather, such knowledge lives in the living, ongoing work of coming to a place, learning its ways, and living with the unforeseeable consequence that you inevitably become someone in such efforts, someone full of tales to tell, tales of intimacy, full of proper names, particular ventures, bodily memories that are entangled in and indebted to the very flesh of the earth they want to tell.

It was clear that my friends loved what they had come to know and what such knowing had required them to become. They took great pleasure in working (Berry, 1988), in showing, in listening, in responding to the simplest, most obvious of questions. There is a telling, disturbing, ecopedagogical (Jardine, 1994) insight buried here. Because a knowledge of the ways of a place is, of necessity, a knowledge webbed into the living character of a place and webbed into the life of the one who bears such knowledge, such knowledge is inevitably fragile, participating in the mortality and passing of the places it knows. A knowledge of ways, then, must, of necessity, include the passing on of what is known as an essential, not accidental part of its knowing. It is always and already deeply pedagogical, concerned not only with the living character of places, but with what is required of us if that living and our living there is to go on.

Another birding lesson: if this place is fouled by the (seeming) inevitabilities of "progress," the cost of that progress is always going to be part of my life that is lost.

Some days, it makes perfect sense to say that all knowledge, like all life, is suffering, undergoing, learning to bear and forbear. Because of this fearsome mortality that is part of a knowledge of ways, we are obliged, in such knowledge, to cultivate a good, rich, earthy understanding of "enough" (Berry, 1987). We are obliged, too, to then suffer again the certain knowledge that in our schools, in our lives, in our hallucinations of progress and all the little panics these induce (Jardine, 1996), there never seems to be enough.

Sometimes, in bearing such knowing, I feel my age. I feel my own passing.

At one point we stood on a raised wooden platform in the middle of a marsh just as the sun was setting, and the vocal interplays of red-winged blackbirds' songs, the curves of their flights and the patterning of both of these around nests cupped in the yellow-and-black-garden-spidery bulrushes—audible but invisible sites bubbling full of the pink, wet warbling smallness of chicks—were clearly, in their own way, acts of spotting *us*.

"Ways" bespeaks a thread of kindredness with what one knows, a sense of deep relatedness and intimate, fleshy obligation (Caputo, 1993). But it betrays another little birding lesson: that we are their relations as much as they are ours, that we are thus caught in whatever regard this place places on us:

> The whole ensemble of sentient life cannot be deployed except from the site of a being which is itself visible, audible, sensible. The visible world and the eye share a common flesh; the flesh is their common being and belonging together. (Caputo, 1993, p. 201)

Or, if you like, a more drastic mosquito lesson about living relations: "Flesh is…a reversible, just insofar as what eats is always edible, what is carnivorous is always carnality" (p. 200). So just as these mosquitoes eat up my sweet, sweaty blood skinslicked under the lures of CO_2 that drew them near, I get their lives in return, gobbled up into liquid gurgling *konk-la-rees*. This is the meaty, trembly level of mutuality and interdependence that crawls beneath all our tall tales of relations. This common flesh is the fearsome limit of our narrativity.

In a knowledge of ways, I do not simply know. I am also *known*. These cicadas and I turn around each other, each forming the other in kind, "both sensible and sensitive, reversible aspects of a common animate element" (Abram, 1996, p. 66). Even more unsettling than this, *as* we know this place, so are we known by it (Palmer, 1989). That is, the character of our knowing and how gracefully and generously we carry what we know reflects on our character.

One final birding lesson for now. Catching a glimpse of a blue heron pair over past the edge of the marsh, tucked up under the willowy overhangs.

Shore edge log long deep bluey sunset shadow fingers.

Sudden rush of a type of recognition almost too intimate to bear, an event of birding never quite lodged in any birding guides:

"It's *that* pair!"

What a strange and incommensurate piece of knowledge (Jardine, 1997a). How profoundly, how deeply, how wonderfully *useless* it is, knowing that it is *them*, seemingly calling for names more intimate, more proper than "heron," descriptions richer and more giddy than "Voice: deep harsh croaks: *frahnk, frahnk, frahnk*" (Peterson, 1980, p. 100) Such knowing doesn't lead anywhere. It is, by itself, already always full, already always enough.

Perhaps this irreplaceable, unavoidable intimacy is why our tales of the earth always seem to include proper names ("obligations require proper names" [Caputo, 1993, p.

201]), always seem to be full of love and heart, always seem to require narrations of particular times and places, particular faces, particular winds, always seem to invite facing and listening and remembering.

It is squarely here that a great deal of my own work has come to rest: how to carry these birding lessons home, back into the often stuffy confines of elementary schools (Jardine, 1990), back into the often even stuffier confines, for example, of elementary school mathematics (Jardine, 1990a, 1995), back, too, into the archaic, often literal-minded narrows of academic work and the forms of speaking and writing and research it allows (Jardine, 1992).

Just imagine: mathematics conceived as a living discipline, a living topography, a living place, full of ancestors (Jardine, 1997) and kin and living relations (Friesen, Clifford, & Jardine, in press), full of tales told and tales to tell. And imagine, too, mathematics education conceived as an open, generous invitation of our children into the intimate ways of this old, mysterious, wondrous place.

CHAPTER *Ten*

Chapter Thirty Two from
"SPEAKING WITH A BONELESS TONGUE"

We are always educating for a world that is or is becoming out of joint, for this is the basic human situation, in which the world is created by mortal hands to serve mortals for a limited time as home. Because the world is made by mortals it wears out; and because it continuously changes its inhabitants it runs the risk of becoming as mortal as they. To preserve the world against the mortality of its creators and inhabitants it must be constantly set right anew. The problem is simply to educate in such a way that a setting-right remains actually possible, even though it can, of course, never be assured. Our hope always hangs on the new which every generation brings; but precisely because we can base our hope only on this, we destroy everything if we so try to control the new that we, the old, can dictate how it will look. Exactly for the sake of what is new and revolutionary in every child, education must be conservative; it must preserve this newness and introduce it as a new thing into the old world. (Arendt, 1969, pp. 192-3)

PEDAGOGY STANDS between invention and tradition, between the young and the old, and it is responsible for both. It provides for the fecund case to deeply meet that *in*

141

the midst of which it might be and remain and show itself as fecund.

This meeting is transformative of tradition as much as it is transformative of the young.

This meeting is *protective* of tradition as much as it is *protective* of the young.

Enamoured of the young alone, pedagogy abandons its responsibility to the world (and falls prey to the "pathos of the new" [Arendt, 1969, p. 178]—the pathos of that which has no sustaining "ethos"). Enamored only of the young, pedagogy, while "worshipping the new," (Hillman, 1987, p. 27) becomes "afflicted by openness," (p. 113) caught up in a headlong "flight into the future," (p. 28) wherein "personal revelation is preferred to objective knowledge," (p. 28) and "wingedness becomes mere haste" (p. 27).

Enamored of the old alone, pedagogy abandons its responsibility to the young (and falls prey to the uninvigorated, merely replicated "ethos of the old," turning ethics into dusty, condescending moralizing). Enamored only of the old, pedagogy becomes "unable to sow seed" (Hillman, 1987, p. 21) and "feeds on the growth of others, as for instance the growth of one's own children," (p. 21) bearing "no wisdom, only knowledge, hoarded in an academic vault or used as power." (p. 21).

Only together are the young fecund (and not simply "new") and is the world set right anew once again (and not simply "old").

The teacher stands along this sharp edge which must move like moontides, pulled by this child and this, attentive, wary, interpreting the world:

> In education [we] assume responsibility for both, for
> the life and development of the child and for the

continuance of the world. These two responsibilities do not by any means coincide; they may indeed come into conflict with each other. The responsibility for the development of the child turns in a certain sense against the world: the child requires special protection and care so that nothing destructive may happen to him from the world. But the world, too, needs protection to keep it from being overrun and destroyed by the onslaught of the new that burst upon it with each new generation. (Arendt, 1969, pp. 185-6)

Arendt goes as far as to suggest that, even in the cases where we may "secretly or openly" (p. 189) wish the world were otherwise, we must, in any case, "stand in relation to the young as representatives of a world for which [we] must assume joint responsibility although [we] ourselves did not make it" (p. 189). (And this right in the midst of all the dangers involved in representationalism—us standing in for the world.) Thus, even in cases where we despise what the world has become, we, as adults, stand before children as co-responsible for what that world has become. The urgency of envisaging pedagogy as involving a generative, ecologically attuned interpretation of the world in such cases is all too obvious. To become responsible for the world means to care for the conditions under which it might now be set right anew—one condition of which is caring for children, for they are one of the irrevocable conditions of renewal.

And this requires deeply understanding, deeply making understandable to children, even those aspects of the world that we might despise, for only to the extent that these aspects of the world become *interpretable* does the possibility of interpreting things differently, "setting right anew," become "actually possible."

At the heart of "teacher-knowledge," then, is the knowledge that the world is interpretable. This is equivalent to knowing that each child is fecund in relation to the world and this is equivalent to knowing that the world itself is multiple and generative in its facets. Believing that the child is fecund is not simply believing that interpretation is *possible.* It is believing that the world *needs* interpretation for its own renewal. And this is not simply loving children for their newness and ebullience and uniqueness, but also loving the world in its full multiplicity, its full, agonizing *interpretability.* If we don't help this child's newness and ebullience and uniqueness work its way out into the world, we abandon the child *and* the world—the child will remain isolated in difference with no soils for sustenance (thereby remaining "unwhole," wound-severed from the world, "puerile," the worst aspect of children) and the world will remain unrenewed (thereby remaining "unwhole," wound-severed from the young and the possibility of its own transformation, "senile," the worst aspect of age).

This is true of us just like it is true of trees who need rooting soils to which they will each in turn add themselves, and soils which need new seeds and roots to burst open layers that are sedimented too hard for bearing.

So, this unbearable Ecopedagogical Wisdom: at the heart of teaching is an agony, not an essence.

So, to make mathematics *livable* (which is *not* the aim of Cartesian logic, believing as it does that mathematics is a self-enclosed, self-referential system, A=A) is to re-introduce it to its agony, its living movement, its character as something one must *suffer* (like Hans-Georg Gadamer's idea of experience-as-suffering or undergoing). It is to link mathematics to pedagogy. Mathematics, if it is to be a living discipline, is always and already pedagogical at its living heart.

Imagine! Disciplines and ways *need* those who will take them on. The specific horror of patriarchal knowledge is the unvoiced belief that this knowledge does not need the young except as mute, identical replicas of itself. These are the "black pedagogies" (Miller, 1989) of "gericentrism" (Smith, 1988). The specific horror of the opposite extreme is the unvoiced belief that earthly wisdoms are not necessary at all, and that all is uniqueness and difference. These are the equally black pedagogies of "pedocentrism" that leave tradition untransformed and unrenewed (but still at work and still powerful now in its worst, most senile aspect the consequence of being left unrenewed, i.e., unread, i.e., uninterpreted). This is the horrible consequence of a phenomenology which will not interpret the world but which moves to an alternate sphere of "lived experience" which it claims is *not* infused by the hardened logics we are living out. Such phenomenology is naïve and dangerous. It works on behalf of the ebulliences of lived experience but will not share in the cultivation of the world within which such experience might be healthily lived out.

Education is the point at which we decide whether we love the world enough to assume responsibility for it and by the same token save it from that ruin which, except for renewal, except for the coming of the new and the young, would be inevitable. And education, too, is where we decide whether we love our children enough not to expel them from our world and leave them to their own devices, nor to strike from their hands their chance of undertaking something new, something unforeseen by us, but to prepare them in advance for the task of renewing a common world. (Arendt, 1969, p. 196).

CHAPTER Eleven

PIAGET'S CLAY AND DESCARTES' WAX

Introduction

IN THE COMMON PARLANCE of Early Childhood Education, children are active learners. They learn and develop by actively engaging in the world, manipulating it, handling it, constructing their own understanding of it in relation to the activities they perform. Each act is taken, quite literally, to be a "making sense" of the world. Knowledge is seen as a construction of meaning; humans are conceived as "meaning makers." On a certain level, this common parlance is beyond doubt. Children learn, grow, and develop by manipulating objects, and in young children, understanding *is* action. And, as a teacher responsible for the education of children, I should provide educationally appropriate materials for such manipulation.

Raising questions about this picture of pedagogy is difficult to do, because it links up, in intimate and often unvoiced ways, with social and cultural presuppositions whose roots extend deeply into Western philosophical traditions and images of the place and function of humanity in the world. It has become commonplace in Western culture to see the world as very little more than a passive, malleable resource for our actions, or as the product of those actions.

147

The language of education, especially that language rooted in the work of Jean Piaget, embodies elements of this picture of the world. The developing child is conceived as an active being whose interactions with the world are acts of "construction." In this view, the world is conceived as the constructive "outcome" of such interactions. The world is something to which we do things, a forum for our concerted action. The world gains its meaning only *vis-à-vis* the structures that the subject can wield to confer meaning on the world. Becoming educated is a matter of developing those structures which ensure that we can act in concert with others in such a conferral of meaning. In Piagetian theory, it means constructing an understanding of the world in light of the "concepts and categories of established science" (Inhelder, 1969, p. 23).

This paper arises out of a vague uneasiness with the notion of understanding as construction and action and the images of mastery, domination, and control that this notion produces. Such images not only emerge in our picture of how children understand the world; they also have come, in some circles, to inform our understanding of the nature of pedagogy itself. The pedagogical act has come to be seen as something we must strategically dominate, manipulate, and control in order to ensure the education of the child (and, of course, to ensure the accountability of the teacher).

It is perhaps inevitable that we would desire to secure, control, and master the path to adulthood for our children, by whatever means possible. As a parent of a five-year-old, I understand this desire most deeply. I want my child to become all that he can become, and I (sometimes desperately) want to have a hand in his becoming, to say the course he takes, to secure his way. However, as an expression of this desire, I have yet to ask clearly how and to what extent

I wish to engender in him an image of understanding as a matter of the constructive and manipulative mastery and control of the world, himself, and others. In the end, I want my child to live a life of his own, a life which goes beyond my mastery and control, both as a parent and as an educator. But more than this, I want to engender in him the possibility of understanding the world, himself, and other people, not as a matter of mastery and control, but as a matter of a sensitive and open engagement with what is "other." I want him to be open to what goes beyond his own constructions, not because he is *forced* to do so (as if what is "other" is inevitably a threat or an enemy of his own constructions, *demanding* accommodation), but in order to preserve what is other as an essential moment in his own self-understanding.

In such an expression of what I hope for my child is an image of pedagogy which does not wish to banish notions of mastery and control as forms of understanding or as goals of education. Rather, mastery and control remain *possible* but not always and everywhere *necessary* forms of Being-in-the-world. It is beyond question that children come to understand the world by actively manipulating it, mastering it, controlling it, and such activities surely have a place, both in our lives and in the lives of our children. However, as educators who are responsible for what children might become, we must ask: What end does this picture of understanding serve? What relationship between the world and being human does this picture engender in the children we teach? In the end, do we want children to become merely manipulative? Do we wish to engender acting without reservation, action held in reserve only when it meets those resistances which, to use Piagetian terminology, *force* it to accommodate them? Do we wish to engender the belief that understanding involves a progressive "conquest of things" (Piaget, 1952, p. 363) and that the world exists only insofar as it is compatible with those methods that wish to conquer it progressively? Even though, given the work of Piaget, this may be what we know children to be, we must face the fact that "all knowledge is nothing more than what we have learned to live with" (Misgeld, Jardine, & Grahame, 1985, p. 203). We must therefore raise the hermeneutic question as to how we have come to live with this picture of pedagogy and what such a picture means for the life we live together with our children.

What follows is simply one thread of this immensely complex issue. It begins by detailing an almost playful coincidence between the work of René Descartes and the work of Jean Piaget, in an attempt to explore one aspect of the origins of our contemporary pedagogical conception of understanding as an active construction of reality. This coincidence is fleshed out with an interpretation of Immanuel Kant's Copernican Revolution. The concluding section is an exploration of some of the images that coalesce around this conception and a reflection on how we might come to give a voice to an alternative to this conception.

Descartes' Wax

Through the process of methodical doubt, René Descartes came upon the *cogito* as that which resists such doubt, as that which is thought with such clarity and distinctness that doubting it is no longer possible. From such a footing, the nature of material objects becomes the focus of inquiry in the *Second Meditation* of his *Meditations on First Philosophy*:

Let us take for example, this piece of wax: it has been
taken quite freshly from the hive, and it has not yet lost
the sweetness of the honey which it contains; it still
retains somewhat of the odor of the flowers from which
it has been culled; its color, its figure, its size are apparent;
it is hard, cold, easily handled, and if you strike it with
the finger, it will emit a sound. Finally all the things
which are requisite to cause us distinctly to recognize it
as a body, are met within it. But notice... (Descartes,
1955, p. 102)

From here, Descartes goes on to detail the changes that
the wax undergoes as it approaches his fire: its odor, color,
figure, size, and shape are changed. It is no longer hard,
cold, or easily handled, and it will not longer emit a sound
when struck.

In the face of such phenomenalistic changes, Descartes
asks, "Does the same wax remain?" (p. 103) His initial
answer is striking in its commonplaceness: "We must con-
fess that it remains; none would judge it otherwise." (p.
103) But what is this "it" that remains? "It could certainly
be nothing of all that the senses brought to my notice, since
all these things which fall under taste, smell, sight, touch,
and hearing, are found to be changed, and yet the same
wax remains." (p. 103)

What is it about the material world that resists change,
that persists against methodical doubt, that can be recog-
nized with clarity and distinctness?

Magnitude, or extension in length, breadth, or depth,
I do so perceive; also figure which results from a
terminating of this extension, the situation which bodies
of different figure in relation to one another, and
movement or change of situation; to which we may

also add substance, duration, and number. As to other
things such as light, color, sounds, scents, tastes, heat,
cold, and the other tactile qualities, they are thought
by me with so much confusion that I do not even know
if they are true or false (i.e., whether the ideas which I
form of these qualities are actually ideas or real objects
or not). (Descartes, 1955, p. 116)

"All which I know clearly and distinctly as pertaining
to this object does really belong to it." (Descartes, 1955, p.
139) And what so pertains is, in the end, this piece of wax
insofar as it is the object of logico-mathematical, scientific
discourse, for as such an object, this piece of wax can be
thought with clarity and distinctness.

Interlude

We must not ignore a central concern of Descartes' work.
What is it that guarantees that the clarity and distinctness
of ideas about an object "really belong to it?" Descartes'
work stands at a fundamental turning point of inquiry co-
incident with the advent of modern science: the emergence
of the subject as a fundamental moment, one might say, a
fundamental *problem*, of understanding the world and what
really belongs to it. The task that faced Descartes is one
that displays a hesitancy about reason and its ability to
take its own clarity and distinctness as foundational. In
spite of such clarity, Descartes is compelled to ask how it
is that the subject and the ideas it thinks with clarity and
distinctness are related to objects themselves, objects independent of the subject. Descartes was not able to rest
with the *cogito* (and those ideas which share in its indubi-

tability) as a fundamental. Rather, the self-evidence of the subject becomes precisely the problem of inquiry. In Descartes' *Meditations on First Philosophy*, it is God who secures the subject's ability to transcend itself and understand the world. Because of Descartes' hesitancy, the ideas of reason fail, in a peculiar way, to form a self-enclosed, self-referential system. Reason still longs for its own transcendence and avoids the pretense of maintaining that such transcendence can be accomplished due to reason itself. Reason still requires an "other" in order to understand itself and its own nature and limits.

The Copernican Revolution

> A light broke upon the students of nature. They learned that reason has insight only into that which it produces after a plan of its own, and that it must not allow itself to be kept, as it were, in nature's leading-strings, but must itself show the way with principles of judgement based upon fixed laws, constraining nature to give answer to questions of reason's own determining. (Kant, 1964, p. 20)

> Accordingly, the spontaneity of understanding becomes the formative principle of receptive matter, and in one stroke we have the old mythology of an intellect which glues and rigs together the world's matter with its own forms. (Heidegger, 1985, p. 73)

Immanuel Kant's *Critique of Pure Reason* (1787/1964) turns away from the question of what "really belongs" to objects independent of the subject and turns to the question of the essential characteristics of reason itself. To the extent that nature gives answer to questions of reason's own determining, it is reason that determines nature as experienced by the subject. Kant is no longer concerned with how it may be that reason can transcend its own questions and come upon that which transcends its constructions. In order to preserve God, freedom, and immorality from the hubris of reason, Kant provided a critique of reason which intended to demonstrate that reason *cannot come upon that which is other than its own determination*. Knowledge is possible only insofar as the categories of reason are applied to the sensible manifold. And the sensible manifold *itself* is enformed by the subject through the forms of intuition: space and time. The categories of reason "really belong" to the phenomenal world, since it is through application of such categories to the sensible manifold that the phenomenal world is constituted as an object of knowledge: "The *a priori* conditions of a possible experience in general are the same time conditions of the possibility of objects of experience." (Kant, 1964, p. 138) Without the enforming activity of the subject, all that the world gives itself to be is a chaos of sensory data. It is the activity of the subject which constitutes this chaos into a cosmos. Kant's work thus revolves around a fundamental distinction between the world "in itself" and the world insofar as it is enformed by the subject. The world "in itself" and what "really belongs" to it become nothing more than limiting ideas which we can *think* without contradiction, but which we can never *know* (Kant, 1964, p. 272).

Independent of their application to sensory experience, the categories of pure reason are nothing other than the analytic *a priori* of formal logic. In their application to the sensory manifold, formal logic becomes a transcendental logic (i.e., a logic whereby the subject transcends itself and comes to understand, not objects in themselves, but objects insofar as they are enformed by that act of self-transcendence). There is thus a peculiarity in this notion of self-transcendence. In the act of understanding some object in the world, the subject comes to transcend itself; but in the act of such self-transcendence, the object is enformed by the subject's activity. The subject thus can come to know essential features of an object which transcends it only insofar as the subject finds, in a sense, what it has already placed there. The analytic *a priori* of logic thus becomes the synthetic *a priori* of our knowledge of the world (i.e., the universal and necessary forms whereby experience is synthesized). For example, hypothetical judgement in formal logic (if A then B) becomes, in transcendental logic, an *a priori* condition of all possible experience: all events have a cause. We may not know the cause of a particular event in our experience (this is a matter of empirical experience), but we know, *a priori*, *that* it has a cause, since this is an essential condition of the possibility of experience itself and therefore an essential form of all objects of experience.

With the Kantian Copernican Revolution, we thus have the opposite movement to that of the discoveries of Copernicus: Copernicus *displaced* humanity from the center of the universe, and Kant's epistemological revolution *re-placed* humanity at the center by making nature answerable to questions of reason's own determining. In such a revolution, nature "in itself" may be preserved from the hubris of reason. But as a correlative to such preservation, the phenomenal world becomes a closed system which has reason as its mater, as that to which this system is answerable. Therefore, the task of scientific knowledge is clearly not to ask after that which might transcend such a closed system. It is not to ask after that which might go beyond its own methodical constructions, which might bring up short its own pretensions to mastery and control. Rather, the task of scientific knowledge is to master and control nature, since it is precisely the terms of such mastery (the categories of reason in their application to sensory experience) which constitute nature in the first place. That which transcends such terms of mastery is henceforth banished to the realm of faith or the idiosyncrasies of subjectivity.

In a peculiar sense, then, mastering nature becomes a form of self-mastery. As long as the human subject can master itself by adhering to the logico-mathematical core of reason—as long as the human subject remains an "epistemic subject"—it remains at the center of nature, because it remains at the center of the questioning to which nature is answerable. Through such adherence, we gain mastery and control over what is as a whole, since we gain mastery over those epistemic conditions which make what is possible at all. And through such adherence, we step decisively into the age of the monologue of scientific discourse (see Habermas, 1973). Such discourse is a monologue in two senses: First, every human subject's voice must speak with the common voice of science if it is to understand the world, since that world is constituted by the categories of such a common voice. Science becomes the repository of the "true." Second, this singular voice can hear no other voice. It is answerable only to itself, to its own inner necessity. It cannot attend to that which goes beyond its own questions since, in its methodical advance, it is precisely those questions which provide the setting in which the world is brought forth "in truth":

Man sets himself up as the setting in which whatever is

must henceforth set itself forth, must present itself. Man becomes the representative of that which is. What is decisive is that man expressly takes up this position as one constituted by himself...and that he makes it secure as the solid footing for a possible development of humanity. There begins that way of being human which means the realm of human capacity as a domain given over to measuring and executing, for the purposes of gaining mastery over what is as a whole. (Heidegger, 1977, p. 132)

Clay

Though tangible matter provides motivity with its reference points and signals, the latter provides it with its structures. Sense data are meaningless unless they are assimilated to repeated actions.(Piaget & Inhelder, 1972, p. 279)

Piaget's work emerges out of the Kantian spirit, but, as he notes, the structures of logico-mathematical knowledge that are fundamental to his theory as the *telos* of development are the *terminus ad quem* (the point to which) rather than the *terminus a quo* (the point from which) knowledge emerges (Piaget, 1965, p. 57). The "*a priori* only appears in the form of essential *structures* at the end of the evolution of concepts and not at their beginning" (Piaget, 1952, p. 3). And the evolution of the structural *a priori* of intelligence is due to the sequential adaptation of the structures of organism-environment interactions to the "functional *a priori*" or the "functional invariants" (p. 2) that characterize those interactions: the functional *processes* of accommodation, assimilation, and equilibration. And:

It is apparent that this invariant will orient the whole of the successive structures which the mind will then work out in its contact with reality. It will thus play the role that philosophers assigned to the a priori; that is to say, it will impose on the structures certain necessary and irreducible conditions. Only the mistake has sometimes been made of regarding the a priori as consisting in structures existing ready-made from the beginning of development, whereas if the functional invariant of thought is at work in the most primitive stages, it is only little by little that it impresses itself on consciousness due to the elaboration of structures which are increasingly adapted to the function itself. (Piaget, 1952, p. 3)

The last part of this passage is the most telling: it is the *functional activities of the subject*, not precisely the *structures* the subject wields in such activity, which constitute the core of Piaget's work. It is these activities or functions which orient the sequential emergence of the structures that are characteristic of each level of development. In fact, Piaget maintains that "[structures] have always seemed to us to be...the products of a continuous activity which is immanent in them and of which they constitute the sequential moments of crystallization" (Piaget, 1952, p. 388).

The structures peculiar to logico-mathematical knowledge form a "higher" level of development in Piagetian theory, not precisely because they are best adapted to some "reality" considered independent of the subject's activity, but because they are *best adapted to the process of adapting itself*, best adapted to the "function itself." With the structures peculiar to logico-mathematical knowledge the *functional* or *operational* character of the organism's interactions with the world are made fully explicit: in scientific discourse, the *structures* whereby we operate on the world are understood explicitly as *ways of operating on the world*. This is why the stage of logico-mathematical knowledge in Piagetian theory is characterized as a stage of logico-mathematical *operations*. At the level of logico-mathematical knowledge, we are dealing with "a closed operational system" (Piaget & Inhelder, 1972, p. 278). We are dealing, in the end, with the *methods* of science. And, as a *method*, science can lay out in advance procedures for dealing with the disruption of the equilibrium it has achieved, it prepares for such disruption by laying out hypotheses which it can test, such that the potential failure of the hypothesis is already a feature of the procedure of laying it out. It can therefore methodically anticipate the inevitable and ongoing process of adaptation. In this way, it forms a "more inclusive and more stable" (Piaget, 1973, p. 7) form of equilibrium than "lower" stages, since it actively anticipates the possible disruption of that equilibrium. This allows Piaget to avoid the pretense of saying that the current state of scientific knowledge "encompasses the whole of reality," (p. 9) while also saying that the process of advancing that state of knowledge (the objective methods of scientific discourse) accomplishes such encompassing by encompassing the functional conditions under which structural change is possible. Scientific method is thus "an *extension* and *perfection* of all adaptive processes" (p. 7) because it crystallizes into an objective methodology precisely the functional *a priori* of those processes.

In Piaget's genetic epistemology, then, reality becomes answerable to the *a priori* functioning of the subject, and it is so answerable at each level of development. The peculiarity of the structures characteristic of scientific discourse is not simply that they make reality answerable to such structures (it shares this in common with all of the functionings of the organism), but that those structures are explicitly articulated to the *process* of making reality so answerable. It is for this reason that Piaget maintains that "the progress of reason doubtless consists in an increasingly advanced awareness of the organizing activity inherent in life itself" (Piaget, 1952, p. 19). For Piaget, scientific method is a pure expression of the organizing activity inherent in life itself. And insofar as this organizing activity is that in terms of which reality is organized, scientific method is precisely that which best expresses the nature of reality. And also, as with Kant, to the extent that one adheres to the organizing activity requisite of scientific discourse, one adheres to the nature of the real by adhering to that discourse which essentially constitutes the real. It is little wonder, then, that Piaget maintains that "the sciences are self-sufficient and alone guarantee their own reflection" (Piaget, 1965, p. 225). Calling upon anything else for that guarantee or that sufficiency would entail turning away from the life out of which science emerges and in which science appears as the extension and perfection of that life. There is thus an "inner necessity" to science, an "intrinsic intelligibility" (Piaget, 1968, p. 5). In its careful and breathtaking advance, it has secured its understanding of the world in methods which can envisage alternatives to such methods only as a breach of this security.

It is against this background that a peculiar coincidence with Descartes' manipulation of a piece of wax occurs in Piaget's work. In *The Child's Construction of Quantities*, by Piaget and Barbel Inhelder (1972), the central problem is "to determine how the child constructs extensive...quantities from...originally phenomenalistic and egocentric qualities" (p. viii). The central question of this text is this: "Is [the child] guided by experience, or by mental constructions of his own?" (p. viii) In order to address these questions,

> the method we shall be using...is extremely simple. The child is handed a ball of modeling clay, together with a lump of the same material, from which he is asked to make another ball "as big and as heavy as the first." Once he is satisfied that the two balls are identical, the demonstrator changes the shape of one of them by drawing it out into a coil (a roll of sausage shape), by flattening it into a disc, or by cutting it up into pieces. He asks the child if the two objects still have the same weight, quantity of matter, volume, etc. The child is expected to justify all his answers, so that it is possible to determine not only whether or not he accepts the idea of conservation but also how he substantiates and elaborates it. (p. 4)

Our concern, at this juncture, is not to detail all of the stages of the development of the child's construction of quantities. Rather, our concern is with the "locale" of the answers Piaget's theory generates.

The task posed by the series of experiments in Piaget's work is clear: How does the child go beyond the phenomenalistic changes of the clay and develop an understanding of what persists independently of such changes (i.e., that the weight, volume, etc., remain identical in spite of phenomenalistic changes)? Is this, as with Descartes' work, a question of what "really belongs" to the clay? No. Rather, once the child realizes that the operations performed on the clay in order to make it into a flat disc can be *reversed*, "perceptive relations have made way for operational relations" (p. 17) such that "identity has become associated," not with properties of the object, but "with *the operations themselves*" (p. 16). The identity of material objects is thus equated with the reversible operations that the subject can *perform on the object*. In a fashion analogous to the work of Kant, the identity of objects of experience becomes a function of the constructive activity of the subject. Substance becomes a matter of the subject's ability to conserve substance; weight becomes a matter of the subject's ability to conserve weight, and so on. What persists in phenomenalistic changes is the operational ability of the subject to reverse such changes and thereby construct ideas of identity, substance, weight, volume, and the like. These become categories into which empirical experience is organized. Thus, for example, the identity of material objects is not the source of our idea of identity, but rather the *constructive outcome* or "result" of the operations of the subject. In short:

> In purely perceptive terms, the coil is not identical with the ball: it is less compact, thinner, etc. Before this idea can be dispelled the data must be elaborated with the help of a system of operations of which identity can only be the result and not the source. (p. 11)

Piaget therefore tells us that his text details the developmental stages in the "intellectual organization of the external world" (p. vii). Questions regarding the nature of the real and our place in it become questions of the *construction of the real* and the development of our ability to *place ourselves* "in it" (Piaget, 1974, p. xi).

Transcending subjectivity is not accomplished by asking after that which exists "in itself," independent of the constructions of the subject, or by calling on God to guarantee that the ideas of subjectivity "really belong" to objects, but by asking after those methods of operation which we share in common with others—the common organizing activity inherent in life itself. "Objectivity does not...mean independence in relation to the assimilatory activity of intelligence, but simply dissociation from the self and from egocentric subjectivity" (Piaget, 1952, p. 366). It means constructing reality *vis-à-vis* "processes common to all subjects" (Piaget, 1965, p. 108).

A distinction must be at once drawn between the individual subject, centered on his sense organs or on his own actions—and hence on the ego or egocentric subject as a source of possible deformation or illusion of the "subjective" type in the basic meaning of the term—and the decentered subject who coordinates his actions as between them and those of others; who measures, calculates, and deduces in a way that can be generally verified; and whose epistemic activities are therefore common to all subjects, even if they are replaced by electronic or cybernetic machines with a built-in logical and mathematical capacity similar to that of the human brain. (Piaget, 1973, pp. 7-8).

The development of the child is thus understood as the development of the child's ability to decenter from egocentric subjectivity and center its activities on the processes common to all subjects, the processes typical of scientific discourse. It is understood as the development of the ability to participate in a common construction of the world. Such an orientation emerges out of the child's persistent activity on objects, persistent accommodation of his or her assimilatory schemata to such activity, and the sequential equilibration/crystallization of such activity into the structures typical of each level of development. Without the activity of the subject, the "world" is a meaningless array of sensory data. "In fact, every relation between the living being and its environment has this particular characteristic: the former, instead of submitting passively to the latter, modifies it by imposing on it a certain structure of its own." (Piaget, 1965, p. 188)

Concluding Reflections of Pedagogy and Understanding as Construction

Education is suffering from narration-sickness," says Paulo Freire. It speaks out of a story which was once full of enthusiasm, but now shows itself to be incapable of a surprise ending. The nausea of narration-sickness comes from having heard enough, from hearing many variations on a theme, but no new theme. A narrative which is sick may claim to speak for all, yet it has no aporia, no possibility of meeting a stranger because the text is already complete. Our theorizing must inevitably become stuck, for then we are no longer available for that which comes to meet us from beyond ourselves, having determined in advance the conditions under which any new thing will be acceptable and thereby foreclosing on the possibility of our own transformation. (Smith, 1986, p. 18)

It is possible to consider the children in Piaget's experiment as the progeny of Descartes, being handed the equivalent of his wax and being asked what "really belongs" to it. Of course, Piaget discovers, against Descartes, that "some *would* judge it otherwise"—for young children,

the same wax *does not* remain. Piaget's work thus traces
the sequential development from the child's developmental inability to judge that the same wax remains to that it
does remain.

But there is a much deeper sense in which the children of Piaget's experiment are the progeny of Descartes,
and there is a profound sense in which they are children
whom Descartes would disown. The children in Piaget's
experiment are the progeny of the *cogito* and the inheritors
of a picture of the world in which nature has become answerable to the methodical constructions of human understanding. Out of Descartes' work emerged the possibility
of conceiving of the subject as a moment of inquiry. And
out of this moment unfolds the unintended legacy of conceiving the world as answerable to the methodical manipu-
lations of the subject, a subject now no longer earthly and
human, but ideational. Understanding becomes a matter of
construction, and self-understanding, in Piagetian theory,
becomes a matter of explicitly setting forth those constructions in terms of an objective methodology. Such a setting
forth houses understanding within the parameters of that
which speaks with a common voice, a common understanding. Such commonness, although it gives rise to the security that flows from repeatability, verifiability, and methodi-
calness, can hear no voice other than its own. As the object
of understanding-as-construction, children are banished
to silence. Even in the act of carefully listening to children, which Piaget's work exemplifies so clearly, the methodical parameters in which we "pigeon-hole" (Piaget,
1965, p. 55) what they have to say is already understood,
already mapped out ahead of time. Listening to children
might give us new empirical information about their conceptions of the world, but it will never put in jeopardy the

methodical constructions in terms of which such conceptions "make sense." Whatever children have to say, that speech must become re-cast as the object of scientific discourse if it is to count. That discourse itself is never put into question by alternate forms of speech since, for Piaget, it is only in the securing of scientific discourse against such disruption that it becomes objective, that it becomes truly scientific. Thus, "the method of modern science is characterized from the start by a refusal: namely, to exclude all that which actually eludes its own methods and procedures" (Gadamer, 1977, p. 93).

Such a monological picture of understanding as operating within its own constructions threatens the foreclosure of understanding to any other voice. In the end, the goal of understanding-as-construction is closure, completeness, mastery, and, in the end, silence, the completion of the pedagogical narrative. In education conceived after a model of understanding-as-construction,

> ideally, research orients to that first articulation of what it means to be a child or an adult about which nothing more needs to be said, about which no further specification is needed or possible, in relation to which every variable has been controlled such that, in the end, research would dispel the need of saying more. Being an adult or being a child would, ideally, become exhausted issues, in need of no further consideration. This accounts for the rather manic and hysterical character of some forms of education research, and the relentless proliferation of "research data" which has disassembled children and adults into the smallest specifiable variables. The impetus of such research seems to be the fixing of the as-yet-unfixed variable, the discovery of which in and of itself warrants further

research. The goal of such research seems to be silence—the end of the need to address such issues. (Jardine & Misgeld, 1989, p. 220)

Orienting to understanding-as-construction, the language of education orients to silence, not as a moment finally to attend to what goes beyond our own constructions, but as an outcome of a universalizing discourse which wishes to exhaust the possibilities of speech, the possibility of saying more.

Clearly in the area of pedagogy, the text is not yet complete. But it is equally clear that we live in a culture which desires such completion. As educational theorists, we live with the cultural desire finally to get the child's curriculum *right* once and for all, to fix our relation to every possible feature of the child's life methodically so that the pedagogical act will not have to live with uncertainty, ambiguity, risk. We will have finally mastered it once and for all. And we often do this without first asking whether such risk, ambiguity, and uncertainty are essential to the character of understanding itself. We live with the frightening prospect that the nature of understanding is in the first place to secure ourselves methodically against the possibility of misunderstanding (Gadamer, 1977, p. 15), as if the breach of understanding were not an ecstatic moment of self-transcendence, wherein we can finally understand something more than just the method we practice. A breach of understanding is not pictured this way. Rather, it is seen as simply a falling away from objectivity and the self-security of method. It is this sort of picture that has led one author (Smith, 1988) to reflect on the militaristic metaphors of contemporary pedagogy. We come to see the teachable moment as the opportunity, not for attending to a particular child, but for gearing up for a surgical strike against children. We come to see threats to teacher accountability not as a moment to reflect on what children might need, or as a call for a pause in the relentless of our active intervention in children's lives, but as a call for the endless proliferation of forms, tests, and charts which will provide us with our own version of a strategic defense initiative—an initiative which will allow us to continue to act and which will allow us to escape the need to reflect on the warrantability of such action. And all the while, we engender this picture of understanding in our children. We engender in our children the same fear of losing ourselves (Gadamer, 1977, p. 51) to something more than our own constructions, that which we can wield to make the world into an object of our mastery and control.

But what is the alternative to understanding-as-construction? We cannot stop this by simply declaring an end to it or being adamantly passive, which simply works itself out as a form of passive aggressiveness and refusal. "Can we find ourselves a position between, on the one hand, a methodological fanaticism which would forbid us to understand anything besides the method we practice, and, on the other, a feeble eclecticism which would exhaust itself in inglorious compromise?" (Ricouer, 1980) We must find a way to help our children ask after what is at stake in action, what is at stake in speech, and this requires a sensitivity to what life situations call for, a sensitivity to what addresses us. What is required is a picture of understanding as dialogical rather than monological. When it is conceived as dialogical, one always begins within the parameters of one's own understanding, one's own experience, one's own constructions. But the goal of dialogue is not simply to reproduce the world in the image of those prejudices, however essential they may be as the point from which understanding begins. It is not to create the world in our own image, but to be open to what we cannot imagine by ourselves. In dialogue, it is essential to listen for another voice and to orient to finding a mutual understanding, a kinship between this voice and my own. There is no methodical standpoint from which mutual understanding proceeds, since it is precisely where I stand in relation to my interlocutor that is at issue in such a search for mutual understanding. An orientation to the dialogical character of education requires something other than relentless action and endless speech. It requires listening, attending, and, very often, silence. It requires envisaging understanding as something other than a form of methodological self-defense where what is "other" or "different," what falls outside my own constructions, is nothing more than an enemy or a threat.

It is implicit hatred of difference that leads to Ricoeur's notion of methodological fanaticism. It is the search for univocity, for one voice, for identity. Univocal speech conceives the act of understanding as a desire to dispel difference: "Difference becomes a problem to be solved and subsumed under a condition of mastery and explanation." (Smith, 1988, p. 4) In such an act, understanding children is to turn them inside-out, to search out every nook and cranny, so that we will no longer be surprised, so there will be no surprise ending, so the narrative will be complete. But the opposite of such subsumption is not the scattering of speech into differences, where every understanding is compromised by being understood as bound by the isolation of "the individual."

In a hermeneutic conception of understanding, identity and difference are not the alternatives. In dialogue with another person, I do not become identical to my interlocutor, but neither can I remain simply different. In dialogue, mutual understanding is sought, but it is sought in such a way that our real differences are preserved while, at the same time, kinships, resemblances, or analogies of understanding emerge. In the area of education, this phenomenon of analogical interrelatedness is especially important. We find ourselves constantly in the presence of those who think differently than we do *and*, at the same time, finding these others as persons whom we wish to engage, to understand, to educate. As teachers, we find that "the full meaning of a child...resides in the paradox of being part of us but also apart from us" (Smith, 1988, p. 4). We find ourselves in kinship with children, belonging together with children, while neither being quite the same or simply different. We find, as teachers, that we must live in the dialogue *between* same and different in which mutual understanding is sought. Effective teachers cannot begin with a refusal: namely, a retreat into their own constructions and the limits of their own strategic action. In the pedagogical act, then, children cannot become the passive object of mastery and control, but neither is this act simply handed over to children as an inglorious compromise with their difference. The analogical character of dialogue lives in a tension between same and different, and understanding is not produced by the dispelling of this tension, but by sustaining ourselves in it. We find, in such an orientation, that "genuine life together is made possible only in the context of an ongoing conversation which is never over yet which also must be sustained for life together to go on at all" (Smith, 1988, p. 4). The other voice thereby becomes a moment in my own understanding and self-understanding. It is only in being open to another voice that I can hear my own voice as authentically my own.

The legacy of understanding-as-construction is deeply engrained in Western culture, and we, as educators, often find ourselves caught up in its relentlessness. It is difficult to imagine that true speech might emerge out of silence, that action becomes exquisite when it is borne out of "inaction"—out of waiting, listening, attending. This requires that we allow that the pedagogical narrative is not complete and that such incompleteness is not a call for more stringent mastery and control, but is an indication of the nature of how we live our lives in relation to children—in an ongoing dialogue which recognizes our inexorable difference from children while expressing ever anew our kinship with children. The pedagogical narrative is not complete, but the narration sickness remains. A hermeneutic conception of the pedagogical narrative as essentially dialogical/analogical may help address this sickness, but we are not dealing here simply with a matter of education theory and practice, but with something much more endemic. As I complete this paper, I find my son working out his understanding of the world, himself, and others through the medium of Masters of the Universe. I think I'll go talk with him. I hope that I can hear what he has to say.

CHAPTER *Twelve*

THE CHILD
OF WRITING

I

MUCH HAS BEEN MADE of the potential violence and imperialism of the act of writing in those times when we take our words too literally, and believe that we, unlike all who have come before, have finally named the gods.

"Literalism is the enemy. Literalism is sickness." (Hillman, 1975, p. 3)

If we read a great deal of educational theorizing, this sickness is rampant. Much educational writing is full of the strange brutalities of literalism, treating children or mathematics or writing or the graceful turns of teacher and child attending with their lives to a text, into objects to be pinned and fixed in words. We so often unwittingly operate with the strange and sad desire to name things once and for all, to tie things up and mute them and force the life from them into objectivities we can control, predict, and manipulate (Habermas, 1973).

This involves not only a misunderstanding of the ways of words, but of the ways of things as well. Heated arguments about who gets to have the final word (Gadamer, 1989, p. 579). The odd hope, especially for education, that we might have articulated the lives of our children and the

173

life of the earth to the extent that nothing more needs to be said, and we can finally raise our children in a strained and violent silence.

This is a standing joke: conversations with teachers, and how you would have thought that, after all these years, after all these journal articles, after all these books, after all this writing, after all these university classes, after all these meetings, after all this effort, after all these marks of age and wisdom borne in the bones and on the flesh, that we would have finally got the curriculum *right* so that we wouldn't have to think about it any more.

Joke.

It tickles a certain humor, a certain sense of humanity, and a certain sense of humility. We already somehow know that our lives and our children's lives and the bristling life of the earth are never simply objects, never simply givens, never simply presences that writing can surround.

Literalism will not do, nor will its correlative belief in the givenness of the lives about which we are writing.

II

At its heart, pedagogy heralds the arrival of new life here in our midst (Smith, 1988). Our children will have something to say about what we have heretofore understood to be the givens in our lives, in theirs, and in our ways of understanding the earth. Disemboweling the obvious.

Pedagogy thus requires "keeping the world open" (Eliade, 1968, p. 139) to this arrival. Such an open world is not literally simply what it is. It is not constituted by objective self-identity, where A=A. It is not simply a given. It has to be made and remade, read and re-read, written and re-written, breathed and borne. It is a *living* earth, this world, animate, full of spooks and spirits, multiple voices beyond the "one voice" (*univoce*) of self-identity. Such a world is open to becoming understood otherwise, to *becoming* otherwise.

Such a world is interpretable. It is *enterable*, full of portals and ways.

Or, inversely put, this is how we depend on the child, for the (re-)opening of the world. "The child" is a herald of an interpretable world. Of a living world.

Pedagogy thus works specifically on behalf of "the child" and the child bursts beyond the literally chronologically young (as it ought, since I am still my parent's child). "The child" becomes a sign, not just an identifiable "thing." "The child" becomes a sign of keeping alive and well and strong the *inability* to name things once and for all.

Just imagine. A pedagogy premised on an inability. Imagine more: that this inability is not a deficit that maturing will fix. We, these formed and fashioned adults, still bear the inability to name things once and for all. We still bear the child in us.

At its heart, then, pedagogy belies literalism—the closing of the case, the final declaration of "this *is* that" (Clifford, 1986, p. 100), where words gobble up things in violent consummation.

A pedagogy that is open to the arrival of the child requires the hermeneutic insight that the whole is never given, only hinted in suspicions of kinship, likeness, verisimilitude.

This is why so much contemporary talk in education is beginning to revolve around the story, the parable whose parabolic lines of words never finally touch what they speak about (never becoming an identity, where "this *is* that"), but simply draw us in, draw us closer.

In parables, we learn from the movement of showing (Heidegger, 1972, p. 1), not from being morally delivered unto "the point." "The child" portends an unpresentable absence, an unfulfillable lack. A movement.

This absence works itself out in the simplest of events. I will never fully understand this piece of a child's work, or this utterance or gesture or look, because I can never fully know what will come of it. It is always "yet to be decided" (Gadamer, 1989, p. 361), always emptying into all its forthcoming relations, always still arriving. The story continues. Just like my son transformed me into a father, and my father into his grandfather, and my father into my father differently than he had been before I had a son of my own.

Just like these kinships and family resemblances (Wittgenstein, 1968), these things we write suffer the fact that life continues. They will be re-read in light of the fleshy course of events.

Literalism thereby is a sickness of denial. It is premised on a fear of the suffering at the heart of life itself, sad desires for a type of permanence in which children—the arrival of the new, the arrival of yet another demand that our theorizing be called to account—are no longer possible except as a problem.

Another way of experiencing the suffering at the heart of life itself is that life is interpretable and finite.

Another old joke: I had my school year planned out perfectly and then the kids arrived, little monsters (Jardine, 1994).

Hermes was often quite a little monster, teasing Apollo and "inciting him to great rage" (Smith, 1991, p. 141).

III

At its heart, one would expect, pedagogical writing—writing that *is* pedagogical, not simply *about* pedagogy—must itself break with the brutalities of literalism. Pedagogical writing must somehow harbor the arrival of the child. Harbor. Prepare a place. Not too literally. The arrival of the opening of the world, of freshness, of ebullience, of naïveté and innocence, of new blood (Jardine, 1996), of renewal, of vulnerability, "are" (but not literally) the arrival of "the child."

Pedagogical writing must harbor the child by keeping the world open. It must operate in a language full of possibilities, for only in a language full of possibilities is it conceivable that things could be understood, named, or uttered otherwise, and it is the portend of things being otherwise—of transformation, renewal, and the odd little halts of breath to breath—that the child brings.

Other wise. Only in a language full of possibilities, full of this spaciousness, is it possible for the new voice to enter in, one of us, new kin who will have her say in who this "us" might truly be.

Every statement we make in educational writing must be able to be read as the answer to a question that could have been answered otherwise (Gadamer, 1989). It must be readable out in to the openness of possibilities for which it has provided a particular articulation.

Pedagogical writing—writing that *is* pedagogical, not simply *about* pedagogy—must be interpretable. It must allow the arrival. Hermeneutics *is* pedagogical (Jardine, 1992).

Our world, in its mortality (Arendt, 1969), relies for its

continuance on being read again through the difference that each child brings. Again, not too literally. This is the agonizing process of "setting [things] right anew" (Arendt, 1969, pp. 192-3) that comes with every generation, defines as well the lightning flash of insight, being struck, being taken aback, having things open that were once closed. *Alethia*. As the child, in its youth, moves against mortality, against *lethia*.

This agony is not a mistake that could be sidestepped with research or writing. It involves a wisdom about finitude and death and suffering and continuance the wondrous fact that we can never fully know what might come of the work we do, what might fully come of these words, written. "The helplessness of the written word" (Gadamer, 1989, p. 369) which Plato took to be its failing is, in its own way, its generative, interpretive strength. Writing, in its helplessness in the face of new readings beyond the author's desire, is already a portend of the child. Our children always outstrip us.

It would be illness to want to correct this living, helpless character of writing—its "living metaphoricity" (Gadamer, 1989, p. 432) that always bubbles up despite any efforts at the closures and finality of literalism. Children keep arriving, even though, for literalism, children are the enemy, children are sickness.

IV

My son *will* rename the world beyond my wanting and willing, and the old ways will groan under his utterance and turn green again, shedding what will no longer do.

But all of this will catch hold only if the renaming is done with an ear to the echoes off the hills, an ear to coyote yelping up our ridge, his moony giggle reminding.

He cannot sanely rename alone, as if the recovery of the child is the recovery of some Enlightenment hallucination of a worldless, autonomous voice, as if ebullience and newness cut loose and abandoned are somehow healthy and whole.

The child arrives *here*, right in the midst of these things, right in the midst of this fleshy earth, full of other voices and desires, full of places and homes and words. Full of relations, for good or ill.

He must eventually give things the names they need, proper names, full of obligation and grace, full of proportion and properness to this place, here, now, in these turns of the events of understanding.

His ebullience must eventually deepen into wisdoms. And wisdoms that have been set down in writing or in tales or in ways must be pliant and generous enough to let his difference arrive. Without him, the wisdoms will not deepen. They are mortal.

Renaming is thus a deeply ecological act. It is not just the arrival of the new. It is the re-opening and transformation of the old and established once again into a living wholeness and health.

Interpretive writing is not simply an enamorment with Hermes the child. It also requires deeply dwelling in the ancestors of the world, the ancients of the earth and, from there, preparing oneself for the arrival, for the "leap" (Hillman, 1991) of difference, of insight.

V

The child "of" writing.
The child born of writing.

The child made visible through the opacities and lacunae of the written word.

The author's child(hood/ishness/likeness).

The child that belongs to and is shaped and formed and cradled in writing.

The child's writing.

Writing's childlikeness.

The child carried down to us in the languages and words and images of the ancestors

> "sedimented layers of
> emotionally resonant metaphors
> revelations of traditions
> recollections of disseminated identities,
> of the divine sparks" (Fischer, 1986, p. 198).

This (child) "of" (writing) is wonderfully ambiguous and otherwise, placed right at the moment of the arrival of the Word:

> Every word breaks forth as if from a center and is related to a whole, through which alone it is a word. Every word causes the whole of the language to which it belongs to resonate. Thus every word, as the event of a moment, carries with it the unsaid, to which it is related by responding and summoning. The occasionality of human speech is not a causal imperfection of its expressive power; it is, rather, the logical expression of the living virtuality of speech that brings a totality of meaning into play, without being able to express it totally. All human speaking is finite in such a way that there is laid up within it an infinity of meaning to be explicated and laid out. That is why the hermeneutical phenomenon can be illuminated only in light of the fundamental finitude of being. (Gadamer, 1989, p. 458)

Interpretive writing writes its way into these moments of "bursting forth," and in doing so, drawing on deep wells. It is deliberately full of (inter) dependence and virtuality, waiting for the ways that the word opens up an unanticipated world of relations. It moves against the illness of literalism's attempts to name things as they are themselves, out of relation to everything else, bristling white-glare actuality that has no possibilities left, no hope, futureless, childless.

Interpretive writing seeks to heal the wounds of lost relations.

It is full of dependents, ancestors, children, and kin.

It is full of "depends."

Children are our dependents and we are theirs and our full dependencies reach wet out into the earth's entrails.

Interpretive writing, *whatever its topic*, invokes the child and invokes the earth not simply as topics which are kept at bay, but as lives which howl in and through our bones and blood.

The nightflutters between the words, dark

Spaces.

Bloody mystery, this.

Writing come alive, a life of its own beyond my wanting and doing (Gadamer, 1989, p. xxvii). The player played.

Like the arrival of Hermes, the young boy, flitting and flirting around, like when a spirited conversation takes off and draws us further. This is why we teach—for this arrival.

All interpretive writing is pedagogical, not because it writes about children but because Hermes flits here, young boy, god of the spaces between, god of the unbridgeable difference between the message and its sender, the message and that which it names, the message and the fateful eyes of reading. It is writing that is drawn out into the mysteries of generativity and renewal, and all the old tales, the parables, that tell us of these things.

And thus, all pedagogical writing is ecological, not because it writes about the earth but because, whatever its topic, that topic is woven out into its dependents/dependencies and rendered otherwise.

Speaking of children without speaking of the earth which embraces their lives and ours is a form of ecological madness.

The earthiness of writing.

Fleshy links.

Full of a certain juice and mystery that leaves wonder in its wake.

VI

The dreamer [who dreams of a child] is not only in charge of the child [lost or abandoned or understood or not understood in the dream]: he also _is_ the child. Consequently, the emotions of worry, guilt and responsibility, morally virtuous as they may be and even partly corrective of neglect, may also prevent other emotions of fright, loss, and helplessness. Sometimes, the more we worry over the child, the less the child really reaches us. So, as long as we take up any dream mainly from the position of the responsible [adult], by reacting to it with guilt and the energetics of setting matters straight, improving by doing, by changing attitudes, extracting moral lessons for the ethically responsible [adult], we [become] further and further remov[ed] from the child. (Hillman, 1975, p. 28)

For me to reach the child (remember the dangers of taking this too literally) and to let him *in* to this world of relations, *in* to this writing (an image of pedagogy), it is not adequate to realize that the child is lost and frightened and helpless and not understood and not understanding, and to write only *in response to that*—desiring to help, to protect, to save, to restore, to understand, to put things right, to clarify, to explain, to comfort, to articulate.

I must also write *out of* helplessness, not just consequent to it and corrective of it—not just *about* it.

I must write out of a forfeiture of understanding, giving up the desire to name once and for all.

The deep disciplines of writing and the wisdoms traced in words—these will return. But they need to know what is needed, and, for this task, they cannot remain steadfast. They are called to attend, to listen to what calls out from beyond our words. *This.*

They are not lost or abandoned but fulfilled in such listening.

Writing out of a forfeiture of understanding means letting the disciplines and traditions and namings I have learned become enlivened by this wind,
>this drop of poplar leaf
>>corkscrewing down in the yellow
>>funnels of air.

The child does not enter into our work in its helplessness by being the topic of a sincere and morally virtuous pedagogy, because sincere and morally virtuous pedagogy does not allow itself and its discourse and its writing to *be* helpless (to *be* "the child" in some full, fleshy sense, a writing full of the flitting knowledge that things could be understood and named otherwise, that the world is interpretable) but rather only *helpful*: it cannot allow *its own helplessness* (its own "child") to become part of the conversation precisely because it gets caught up in its need to be helpful, to do what is right.

Such principles thus remain steadfast (a literal version of "adult" and "mature") and untransformed by the fecund new case (Gadamer, 1989; Jardine, 1992).

Thus steadfast, sincere, and morally virtuous pedagogical principles do not *need* the child except as an instance to which they can be morally and virtuously applied without, of course, the child's interruption.

Thus the old remains firm and fixed and unrenewed, refusing to face its own mortality with grace.

(Letting the child in requires an understanding of death.)

And such "mature" writing turns to pale desecrations, lifeless theories and earnest recommendations, fixated on the young but frustrated by its own inability to admit its need, its own erotic desire, to flirt near the flame, to taste new blood.

This is the reason for the terrible potential violence of a pedagogy that writes only out of a "resolve to take better care of the new and tender parts that need our help to grow" (Hillman, 1975, p. 10).

Such resolute writing cannot let itself be (in a conversation with its own) helpless(ness)—it cannot hear or see past its own resolve.

It is not precisely that we must forfeit such resolve, that we must *become* "the child"—we have only been incited to become *like* unto children, admitting our likeness, our kinship. Admitting that we ourselves, especially as teachers, are deeply constituted by the difficult conversation *between* the young and the old, holding both to account in the work of living our lives well. Deeply drawn into the renaming and remaking of the world.

Hermes arrives in interpretive writing, but still, his words must be understood. There is work afoot. Not just the swoon of insight that Hermes induces, but the age and wisdom to hold such insight. Hermes himself never learns, never ages. The writer does, lines inscribed on flesh, in the deepening of the eyes. I *become* someone in doing this work, now, because of this age, better able than I was to hold the adult and child together.

VII

Interesting to have written such a piece and set it loose, not knowing what might come of it.

Writing as a form of real spiritual work, of the formation of character. Writing has its own helplessness, its own suffering the tides of not being able to be saved by its author. Like the child who must needs venture, strong and measured steps beyond my wanting and doing.

This piece can now be read other wise. Like my son living his own life.

Living a life of his own, a life that somehow once passed through my hands and heart.

How is my child? Is he happy and well? Is he living a life that helps life be lived well?

Hard questions to pose to what could count as educational research.

Hard questions, written, and me now living with the consequences and loving this inability.

All the more strange now that he has slipped from my hands, turned and ran up the wet green hills.

Thirteen

IMMORTALITY
AND THE GESTURE
OF WRITING

I

IN THE BEGINNING PAGES of his novel *Immortality* (1990), Milan Kundera does what he will do for the remainder of that work—he plays lightly and delicately with his own authorship, treating it like the fictitious figure of Agnes who figures as one of the main characters of the text.

Kundera begins by describing an old woman leaving the side of a swimming pool and how out of her light and delicate gesture of farewell—"as if she were playfully tossing a brightly colored ball to her lover. The charm of a gesture drowning in the charmlessness of the body" (Kundera, 1990, p. 3)—precipitates a much younger woman, Agnes, who becomes a central figure in the novel and whose friends and lovers re-intersect with "Kundera himself" at the novel's end in long and swirling debates about "gestures" and their precipitations.

This old woman seems sacrificed by the writing. She seems left behind as an ephemeral trace, never to exactly

re-appear. Perhaps only appearing at the novel's beginning purposefully to leave her behind.

No. Wait. Say this again. Kundera purposefully left in
these traces as part of the text. We are left, not only with
Agnes, but with the unforgettable memory trace of how she
appeared, at what cost, small traces left of this "real" old
woman who was, of course and after all, herself simply a
figure in these fictions of immortality.

Just as is this purposeful author Kundera who witnesses
her and her gestures by the pool. A figure composing itself
in these fictions of immortality: a good description of the
desires of writing and the nature of authorship.

Shall we then understand the body of the old simply as
the occasion for the young's remembrance and their vain
precipitations? It is often this way with charming little in-
cidents in interpretive work: charming, fresh scrubbed
young boy Hermes arrives, full of piss and vinegar, full of
thievery, so that even if this old woman protested and said
"that's not what I meant at all, not at all," (Hillman, 1989),
it would already be too late, since Kundera (1990) "himself" already has written:

> That smile and that gesture had charm and elegance,
> while the face and the body no longer had any charm.
> It was the charm of a gesture drowning in the
> charmlessness of the body. The essence of her charm…
> revealed itself for a second in that gesture and dazzled
> me. I was strangely moved. And then the word Agnes
> entered my mind. Agnes. I had never known a woman
> by that name. (p. 3)

These damn authors! "Whether we listen or not won't
stop them from telling our story in their own." (Wallace,
1987, p. 48)

So, are Kundera's thievery and his gestures of writing meant to be a bit of a gift of immortality? Or at least "making memory last" (Gadamer, 1989, p. 391) a bit longer than the stretch of failing days? Because, like with the gestures of writing that left that old woman behind, in remembering, there must be forgetting, forgiving, forgrounding:

> forgetting is closely related to keeping in mind and remembering; forgetting is not merely an absence and a lack. Only by forgetting does the mind have the possibility of total renewal, the capacity to see everything with fresh eyes. (Gadamer, 1989, p. 15)

So perhaps the gestures of writing are a way of rushing ahead of the frailties and burdens of the sometimes charmless lives we live and opening us up to some fluidity and moistness against the fixities and dryness of age (Hillman, 1987).

We could expect no less from the piss-and-vinegar puerility of a boy like Hermes. Fresh Eyes.

Offering a deeply human understanding: a remembering (*alethia*) that embraces a necessary forgetting (*Lethe*). So that who we become is thus always the twinning of what memory holds with what forgetting leaves behind.

In writing, we compose ourselves.

II

My father died in the summer of 1992. And when my brother and I returned to our parent's house to find him hospitalized and comatose, we also found something almost even more bewildering. There, our mother, now finally freed from him and all the wonderful, odd and frightened things that he was.

All those things that have already fled as blood blossomed in his skull and his body drooped wet and warm and breathheaving, heavy, heavy.

Tubular lungsuction, hotcloth washings, and all the other tender violations of nursing *caritas*.

And the phone rings at home, and my mother springs up with the cadence and step of the girl she was before they met, having to *be* that one now, self-reliant, a little frightened and confused, but full of a lightness and grace, this gesture, charm released like a flighty little bird, only to be captured again, eventually, in the weight of her years.

Bodily remembrance of a younger woman precipitating out of her old fleshy gestures, like tossing a ball, her lover, now seemingly absent even though, brutally, *there he is*, pulling wet, labored airs in the clean and white surroundings.

And, as she rises for the phone (perhaps "the call" from the hospital), who steps up but one of the Terriault girls— Reta Lenore and sister Fanny Blanche Orlie—up to the lake for a Saturday Dance, some hot and humid Ontario late summer cicada evening, Jackson's Point, 1938.

Duke Ellington and his Orchestra doing "Prelude to a Kiss" by request.

Hoping Bill is there. Fresh Eyes.

III

This spooky little miracle of the appearance of my mother as a young girl faded soon enough into the stubborn events of 1992 and my father's dying. She and I returned to the weight of the world, pulled by its faint and subtle and relentless gravities.

But the essence of her charm...revealed itself for a second in that gesture and dazzled me. I was strangely moved. And then, now six years later, the phrase Immortality and the Gesture of Writing entered my mind.

Immortality and the Gesture of Writing. I had never written a paper by that name.

CHAPTER *Fourteen*

LEARNING TO LOVE
THE INVALID

The issue isn't finding new terms to replace old terms.
The old terms are fine. It's a matter of seeing the old
terms differently, shifting away from both nominalism
and realism to rhetoric and metaphor. (Hillman, 1991,
p. 42)

HUMAN ENCOUNTERS with suffering and with illness are inherent in nursing practice, and nursing, as a
practice profession is often played out in the heart of encounters of illness and infirmity. To be infirmed means to
be weak, ill, or feeble, but it also means to be "not secure
or valid" (Neufeldt & Guralnik, 1988, p. 692). Family
nursing has witness to times when suffering and infirmity
creep into the lives of families, and in this witnessing, nurses
have the daunting and yet tender task of finding room to
accept and love the infirmed, to embrace the invalid, and
to care for the family where what was once valid and healthy
is now challenged and dis-eased with illness. As an expression and understanding of this practice of loving the
invalid, nursing has a innate affinity between its own the
tradition and philosophy of care which resonates strongly
with the traditions and practices of interpretive inquiry and
its openness to difference and to the invalid.

The question of "validity" has been directly inherited

into the discourse of interpretive inquiry from its sister project, quantitative research. Thinking through such complex and rich inheritances can be valuable moments in the establishment of a sense of good work in interpretive inquiry. It can provide glimpses of the often mixed, often contested ancestries of such work, insights into its nature, its origins, its cultures, its limits, its desires, and its differences.

It will come as no surprise, however, that, if interpretive inquiry is to embrace such inheritances, its embrace will, of necessity, be interpretive. By taking up the question of "validity" interpretively, interpretive inquiry will appear, from outside of the orbit of that work, to always appear to be presuming what it ought to be somehow straightforwardly proving, declaring, or showing. It will read as an open, generous, complex, troublesome, multivocal sign what is usually read, in quantitative work, as an issue of a methodo-mathematically fixable relation between one's claims and that about which one is making claims.

In this chapter, I explore how "validity" might come to be a vital, living, *substantive* issue within the rich confines of a place already inhabited, of its own inner necessities, by images and understandings of "the invalid." The rich and living field of nursing requires, in its own practice, learning to love the invalid. Therefore, if it is to do justice to its own inner necessities, it must re-think what place "validity" and "invalidity" might have in it own research pursuits into that practice.

Of course, this is an interpretive formulation of the nature and tasks of nursing, and it may seem, at first, to be merely playing with words—some sort of near-monstrous exaggeration of the etymological rootedness of "validity" in images of value, wholeness, healing, and health. It may portend a monstrous vision of turning our backs on the invalid, despising them, fearing them, shunning them, feeling the creeps of our own mortalities and feeling, too, the unbecoming, ungenerous brazenness of some research endeavors which cannot love the invalid. This playing with words counts, however, as "merely" only if we assume that the literal, definitional, methodological usages of "validity" in research are somehow privileged and beyond question, and, moreover, that living fields of human life can only mutely submit to such literal usages.

Interpretive inquiry wishes to engage with the field of nursing in a substantive, image-filled, topographical (Gadamer, 1989, p. 20) conversation about what is at work in that place (*topos*) beneath the often charming, confidence-inspiring, methodologically secure, literal surface givens of much research into that field. Interpretive inquiry, in fact, deliberately goes looking for "exaggeration" (Gadamer, 1989, p. 115) and the monsters (Jardine, 1994; Jardine & Field, 1992) such exaggerations invoke, because such monstrosities often contain precisely the portends, the demonstrations, the lessons that are needed to be learned or the warnings (*monere*) that need heeding (Chua-Eoan, 1991).

Clearly, then, as a partner engaged in such a conversation in the field of nursing about its wisdoms and its ways, interpretive inquiry is never simply a distanced or disinterested provocateur or an offerer of the procedural "how tos" of interpretation. Interpretive inquiry has its own body (of work), its own stake in the workings of the world, its own desires for health and wholeness, for understanding and for truth. It has, in short, its own life-history, its own tale to tell, its own ancestors and children for whose health it is, in part, responsible.

Interpretive inquiry is thus itself, in its own way, a living topography, inhabited by a rich, complex, contested, substantive images of the workings of human life, a topography which bears, at the outset, a deep inner affinity to the life and understandings and discourse of nursing: health (Gadamer, 1996a, 1996b); healing (Hillman, 1989; Jardine, 1992b); wholeness (Gadamer, 1989); care (Heidegger, 1962; Wilde, 1996); strength and weakness (Gadamer, 1989; Hillman, 1987); life (Gadamer, 1989; Husserl, 1970; Jardine, 1995); time and its pace and passing (Heidegger, 1962; Jardine, 1996b); helplessness (Gadamer, 1989); finitude (Gadamer, 1977, 1989; Heidegger, 1962; Merleau-Ponty, 1965); self-loss and recovery (Gadamer, 1977); embodiment (Merleau-Ponty, 1965); flesh (Abram, 1996; Jardine, 1997; Merleau-Ponty, 1968); wounds (Hillman, 1987; Jardine, 1992a, 1992b); blood (Jardine, 1996a); carnality (Caputo, 1993; Jardine, 1992a; Merleau-Ponty, 1968); edibility (Caputo, 1993; Synder, 1990); generativity (Arendt, 1969; Smith, 1988); familialness (Hillman, 1982); familiarity (Heidegger, 1962); and "family resemblance's" (Jardine, 1992a; Wittgenstein, 1968); natality (Arendt, 1969); mortality (Gadamer, 1996c); death (Heidegger, 1962); and the wisdoms, sufferings (Gadamer, 1989), and "painful [and inevitable] imperfects" (Gadamer, 1989)—or "original difficulties" (Caputo, 1987; Jardine, 1992c), "primary paradoxes that humans must learn to live with" (Snyder)—of human experience and human life.

Clearly, then, in a conversation with the field of nursing, interpretive inquiry will never simply produce claims about that field from some impervious methodological standpoint. Since, as the above citations suggest, interpretive inquiry *already dwells* in the territory of the invalid, it will

also *be laid claim to by the living field of nursing* and, in
relations of intimate exchange, its own understandings, its
own questions, its own images, its own desires, its own limits, its own body (of work) will be read back to it from that
place. "We can entrust ourselves to what we are investigating to guide us safely in the quest." (Gadamer, 1989, p.
378) As if we ourselves were invalids, in interpretive inquiry, we must entrust ourselves to the touch, the feel, the
sensuous presence, the comforting voice of what we desire
to understand. Interpretation thus seeks out the truths that
occur between us (Smith, in press), "expressions of affinity" (Gadamer, 1983): moist and rich and dark and earthy
and embodied "borderings."

Interpretive inquiry does not get to say all by itself what
proceeding generously and attentively and well in this place
of nursing might require of it and therefore, "validity" can
never be a prescribable methodological feature of such work
which the "researcher" can somehow decide upon alone or
in advance. Differently put, "validity" in interpretive inquiry is always dependent upon, always vulnerable to, the
voices it engages, the gazes or gentle looks it comes under
in its work.

Differently put again, its "validity," its "health and
well-being" is never a given but is open to the unforeseeable comings and goings of the world. "Validity" will always have to be worked out once again, here, in this place,
with these faces and beckonings. Understanding, then, is a
contingent, negotiated *venture* to understanding *something*
in the face of and in conversation with others who themselves dwell in a real, bloody, living place, full of its own
spooks and spirits desiring articulation.

Moreover, as much of the above-cited work attests, interpretive inquiry is also, in part, fashioned out of a struggle

to critique the indiscriminate totalizing of objectivistic images of knowledge, and the "surreptitious substitution" (Husserl, 1970, p. 110) of the clean results of objective inquiry for the often unclear, contradictory, marginalized voices roiling underneath such clarities. It thus parallels the struggle of nursing to recognize itself and articulate its place and its character in the face of other threads of the medical profession. As with interpretive work, nursing seeks out and remains near the *body*, the embodiment of knowledge (Merleau-Ponty, 1965) (quite pointedly, the *life*-world [Husserl, 1970]) and the troublesome, pleasurable work involved in working out what is called for, what is known, what might best be done or said in the face of *this* patient's plea, or *these* medical presentations, or *that* sidelong glance of family members.

There is thus this first affinity between interpretive inquiry and the field of nursing. Both recognize an irremediable, ongoing, negotiated, multivocal dis-ease in the day-to-day living of one's life with others and in the attempt "right here, in the midst of things, the whole family listening," (Wallace, 1987, p. 111) to understand, to inquire, to "research" this dis-easy life and not betray its troubles. Both nursing and interpretive inquiry thus face, in their own way, the task of learning to face, learning, in fact, to love this odd, irremediable "invalidity" that is inscribed at the heart of human life.

So, when Hans-Georg Gadamer (1983, p. 48) tell us that "understanding is the expression of the affinity of the one who understands to the one whom he understands and to that which he understands," perhaps the great affinity, the great "bordering," the great "relation," the great "family likeness" (Fowler & Fowler, 1964, p. 22; Wittgenstein, 1968) between interpretive inquiry and nursing is precisely an embrace of the invalid, the finite, the failed, the irremediably "incomplete" (Gadamer, 1989). Forgoing visions of eternity. This is also about us, as family members. Perhaps when we admit this of ourselves, our research into this life might begin to contain a hint of commiseration, of compassion, and of perhaps forgiving these invalids their vulnerability and partiality—their humanity—through admitting our own.

.

CHAPTER *Fifteen*

WALKING
IN THE PURE LAND

If I had supernatural power, I could take you up to the Pure Land of Amitabha Buddha...But once you were there, how would your footsteps be? Can you be sure that your footprints in the Pure Land would not show traces...? To deserve the Pure Land, you must be able to take peaceful steps right here.

If you could take those peaceful...steps while walking on earth, there would be no need for you to go to the Pure Land. When you are peaceful, joyful and free, samsara is transformed into the Pure Land, and you don't need to go anywhere. Then, even if I had supernatural power, I would not have to use it. (Thich Nhat Hanh, A Guide to Walking Meditation, 1985, p. 11-13)

I CAME UPON THE WORK of Thich Nhat Hanh in 1989, almost by accident, while teaching a summer course at the University of Victoria on Vancouver Island.

Over the intervening years, I have been taken, again and again, by how passages in Hanh's work were, on first readings, almost annoyingly simple, especially for an academic well-trained in the convolutions of Kant, Husserl,

Heidegger, Gadamer, and Piaget, and with a head full of the signifying swirls that constitute the doing of hermeneutics as an art within the academy, caught at the center of clamoring voices, trying, sometimes desperately, to remain calm and clear...

...and how, suddenly and without warning, certain things from Hahn's work blossom, ideas and images and words return, seemingly of themselves, always, it seems, just at the right time, as if these words themselves were waiting and watching and mindful of the movements of breath and attention.

As if these words were little trickster-dharma gods, peeking around tree trunks, or out from the grains of splitpine ruddiness and stupor smells and sweats of woodcutting for winter—little gods waiting patiently with lessons.

Spooky to think of images and words (and perhaps even the disciplines we are entrusted with as teachers) being like haunting gods in an animate world (*living* disciplines, curriculum *vitae*), full of their own ancestries, full of their own potentialities and powers and desires. Because after having been read and seemingly forgotten, they sometimes return, seemingly of their own "wanting and doing" (Gadamer, 1989, p. xxviii)—they "come to mind," suggesting a sort of ecopedagogical agency in the world(s of words and images, not just the earthy world of critters). An agency that, if we are ready, if we are alert, *teaches*.

In such teachings, when words like those cited above re-appear and *speak* and *bear witness to themselves* ("Look, here we are" [Hillman, 1982, p. 77]), they are not exactly themselves any longer.

They have retained their simplicities, but they seem to have grown teeth.

They bite, slowly, quietly, and without warning, in places of pleasure, in the writing heart, in the writing breath, in the gestural movements of hands through words. Clearly, then, "understanding begins when something *addresses us*" (Gadamer, 1989, p. 288). Clearly, too, such understanding moves and lives beyond the limits of some odd Protestant-psychologistic hallucination of "subjectivity." When we are addressed, we can glimpse that "the focus on subjectivity is a distorting mirror." (p. 276).

So, then, considering Hahn's cited words, how does my own work rely upon things going or being wrong? How much does my own work seek out how these schools, these teachers, that student-teacher, this curriculum guide, are each not yet the Pure Land? What would I do for a living if these things went away? How much of my writing and work is contingent upon things being amiss? How much do I feed this amiss to keep my own work alive?

What would I do with myself if my dreams came true?

It is not whether such healings are or can be or will be really or ideally possible, or what are the real or ideal conditions that give or block this or that person's or thing's access to such healings. It is also not a matter of whether such healings are naively conceived or seem impractical or ignorant of the "real world." (Such debates have their own necessities and urgencies). It is about whether such healing might—at least in part—require acting and breathing and writing and treating myself and others and this earth *as if the healing had already happened.*

And it's about this. I do not have the strength or the character to walk in the world this way. I need to seek out solace in wild places away from human "wanting and doing."

Places where this "as if" nearly disappears, out catching some winterbreath by the elbow. Feeling, fleetingly, hale.

Snow's coming. You can smell it.

Endbit

Some people say that in the Pure Land there are valuable lotus ponds, seven-gem trees, and roads paved with gold, and that there are special celestial birds. I don't think I would like these very much. I would rather not walk on roads paved with gold and silver. Dirt roads with meadows on both sides are my favorite; I love pebbles and leaves covering the ground. I love bushes, streams, bamboo fences, and ferries.

When I was a young novice, I told my Master, "If the Pure Land doesn't have lemon trees, then I don't want to go." He shook his head and smiled. (Thich Nhat Hanh, A Guide to Walking Meditation, 1985, p. 15)

CHAPTER Sixteen

UNABLE TO RETURN
TO THE GODS
THAT MADE THEM

The sound of water implies...the eye and the ear of a recluse attentive to the minute changes in nature and suggests a large meditative loneliness, sometimes referred to as sabi: the sound of the water paradoxically deepens the sense of surrounding quiet. (Shirane, 1996, p. 51)

L ATE MAY, FOOTHILLS of the Rocky Mountains, and the banks of the Elbow River are starting to shift again under the weight of water and the billow of spring runoff. Funny how the banks and shores and waters and airs have, once again, in this mysterious perennial arc, attended each other so perfectly. *Not one stone*, however meticulously small, is anywhere at all except exactly where it should be, perfectly co-arising in a big, goofy, Alberta sunblue grin of interdependence.

Things have warmed up enough that you can start to smell the pine trees. Evening grosbeaks and pine grosbeaks and red crossbills. Sickly new apsenleaf sour smell. I remember these smells. *But this is not quite right.* This place has taken perfect care of a bodily remembering that I had since forgotten. This place spills my own most intimate memory out into an earthbody greater than this sheath of skin.

Memory, here, alludes to a deep mutuality with this place. I remember these smells, then, but not singlehandedly.

A mating pair of harlequin ducks in a bit of a stillpool on the far shore up against warm cliff-faces.

We've been spotted!

But we'd already been spotted by the aspensmells. Not the Great Alertness of this duck eyeing. But still *there*. A felt awareness of being placed by this place into place in a way I could not have done alone, could not have even imagined.

How can it be that none of these things is ever elsewhere than *precisely* where it is, following the silent mysteries of the ways of water and steepness and volume or the tangled clutters of bushwillowy roots that hold just like *so*, with their long trailing underground reddish rootedness through loose gravel shoals holding as fast as is possible and no faster? How is this possible, that their attentions to all their relations are so acute?

Some have endured this winter's end.

Some have passed and got pushed up onto silty bars or edges alongside a downed age-old spruce whose banksoils failed and in such failure did precisely what was possible. There can be no grieving here except for that sweet fact that all life is One Great Suffering, One Great Undergoing, One Great Passing.

In the presence of such a fact, there is the fragile beginnings of a release from the odd self-containedness, the odd, desperate and understandable holding-on—holding ourselves away from the fact of suffering—that we humans have hallucinated as self-identical substances.

As René Descartes says in his *Meditations on First Philosophy* (circa 1955), "a substance is that which requires

nothing except itself in order to exist" (p. 255). An ecological nightmare, this simple step of envisaging that the
reality of something, its "substance," is what it is independently of everything else, any of its relations, any of its
sufferings. So clearly the great Cartesian task of understanding the substance-reality of any thing is the great task
of severing its relations and forcing it to stand alone under
the colonizing gaze of objectivism (Jardine, 1992c), a gaze
which demands of things that they "shape up" and conform to the logico-mathematical certainties that modern(ist)
science demands of all things. This is one more step along
a path (Jardine, 1990, 1998), inherited by Descartes from
Thomas Aquinas, and before him Aristotle, towards what
biologist E.O. Wilson has named the new era: Nemozoic,
the Age of Great Loneliness.

But this is not the loneliness of a great, empty (*sunyata*)
spaciousness full of dependent co-arisings (*pratitya-
samutpada*). It is not the meditative loneliness of *sabi* which
is aimed at the increase of such releasing spaciousness
around the restlessness paranoia of any seemingly isolated
thing (think, for example, of Chogyam Trungpa's [1990]
"restless cow" image of meditation and the meditative task
of making its meadow larger and larger and richer and richer
"so that the restlessness becomes irrelevant" [p. 44]).

Rather, this is the venerated Protestant-Eurocentric-
Neo-North American Loneliness of Individuality, of one's
self existing estranged of all its relations (like some independent, immortal soul caught through some awful accident in the messy, bloody, dependent squalors of the flesh).
Following from such a sense of estrangement, we then demand such isolationism of earthly things if they are to be
properly and substantially understood, thus reproducing
our own loneliness in all things. A perfect example is an

isolated "math fact" on a Grade One worksheet: "5+3=
__," isolated from the "x" that would make it sensible
(Jardine & Friesen, 1997), isolated from subtraction that
would make it meaningful, memorizable but never especially memorable. A horrible little thing—one more "wanting and doing" (Gadamer, 1989, p. xxviii)—that only needs
to be *done*. Little wonder that a Grade Seven boy recently
told me that he used to want to get his mathematics questions correct "because if I do, I won't have to do any more."

I have never heard a more damning condemnation of
what schools can sometimes (seemingly unwittingly, wit-
lessly) do.

In beginning to release ourselves from such
self-contained holding-on, we necessarily begin to release
ourselves to suffering, to undergoing, to experiencing each
thing (even things like [seemingly] isolated math facts) as
in the earthly embrace of every other, one Great Dharma
Body, turning, wheeling. It is little wonder we rarely pursue such release and enjoy the full consequence of its sweet
and sensuous spell, because this spell portends our own
suffering, our own shit and piss mortalities.

This is the sweet agony of interpretation: every thing
thus begins to appear as a luscious, spacious,
standing-in-itself moment of repose in the midst of a great
and heralded topography of relations and dependencies and
belongings. With the grace of interpretation, we begin to
stand in the vertigo of the movement of "opening," of "clearing." And yes, even that little math fact that seemed so
lifeless, so inept, so isolated, so unmemorable, starts to
howl with the "multifarious...voices" (Gadamer, 1989, p.
284) of all its lost ancestors.

More fearsome yet is the glimpse we suddenly get that
this previously seemingly isolated little math fact *is* that

multifariousness, and to the extent it is presented to our children as an isolated "fact," understanding its real, earthly *facere*, its real "make up" is no longer possible at all. We can only understand this riveredge in the middle of its attunement to and thereby witness of the waters and skies that it has endured. It *is* its endurances, just as we are ours, just as Pythagorean theorem is the attentions it has deservedly endured in order to have come down to us thus (the real mathematical question to ask of Pythagorean theorem is thus not "how do you do it?" but "how has it come to be entrusted to us?" and "*now* what are we going to do?").

Thus I become visible, here, too—"[my] self in its original [earthly] countenance" (Nishitani, 1982, p. 91). Spotted, smelling aspens and also sniffed on passing winds *even if I don't know it*. In the midst of all these things "claiming, *but not requiring* [my] witness" (Hillman, 1982, p. 78).

Spring moon crouched here near river vents that breath when waters roll over rocks and capture oxygens from airs above.

These places of song, where rivers sound. Perfectly so, just like the arcs of rock and the drumskins of waters over white turbulences allow.

In places like this, the old Zen adage finally makes some sort of sense, some deeply bodily sense in the wet middles of this deep earthbody: that if this twirl of dust bootkicked up off the path did not exist, *everything* would be different.

Suddenly, this odd crown of human consciousness gets turned around, turned inside out, caught in the giddy belly giggle of how wonderfully ridiculous is this dribbling trail of words.

This is, of course, the great *converse* that is at the center of a true conversation, that we are turned around: addressed, not simply addressing ("Understanding begins when something addresses us. This is the first condition of hermeneutics." [Gadamer, 1989, p. 299]); claimed (p. 127), not simply making claims; spotted, witnessed, not simply bearing witness: "Not what we do or what we ought to do, but what happens to us over and above our wanting and doing." (p. xxviii) This animate upsurge of the worldbody (not precisely an "unmotivated upsurge" as Merleau-Ponty suggested in an early work [1962, p. xiii], but an upsurge surely beyond the horizon of merely human motivation) is one of the greatest and most fearsome insights of David Abrams' beautiful work (1996).

No. Perhaps the greatest and most fearsome is the moment of knowing I am this earthbody *and nothing besides*.

My consciousness that turns this attention here and there is not different in kind from the lure that pulls these flowerheads to face the sun.

Sit squat in the open forest arc. Spending my passing days listening to the eerie auditory spaciousness of Grosbeak whistle echoes off the foothill to the west.

The ear of the other animal was always already open and even though I'd forgotten to listen, I've been heard.

I sit flower-headed facing sun.

Pulled now, beyond my wanting and doing, into an effort, these words, at airbubble rockcast riversinging.

II

The unnoticeable law of the earth preserves the earth in the sufficiency of the emerging and perishing of all things in the allotted sphere of the possible which everything follows and yet nothing knows. The birch tree never oversteps its possibility. It is [human] will which drives the earth beyond the sphere of its possibility into such things that are no longer a possibility and are thus the impossible. It is one thing to just use the earth, another to receive the blessing of the earth and to become at home in the law of this reception in order to shepherd the mystery and watch over the inviolability of the possible. (Heidegger, 1987, p. 109)

The thing is, I've been living under a hood of depression and distraction and exhaustion for the past months. Somehow, somewhere, I've lost track of the things that might sustain my life, sustain this writing, this *entheos*, things like stomping along this riveredge and feeling my breath surge up again out from under winter's dark dip.

How is it possible to forget such things? Worse yet, how is it possible to forget such things *again*? No sense pretending that this hasn't happened before, feeling a bit like a dirty little math fact caught in perpetual self-isolation. Loneliness. So here's the riverbanks and waters remembering all their living relations exactly, remembering the pitch of aspen smells, with an exquisiteness and a relentlessness and an inviolability that is sometimes almost terrifying, and I'm left, goofing again, forgetting again, fumbling again.

Thank the gods at least that Hans-Georg Gadamer (1989, pp. 15-6) reminded me that the dialectic of memory and forgetting is part of what constitutes the building of character, what constitutes the great and terrible human enterprise of becoming *someone*. This is why the first part of his *Truth and Method* speaks so often of *Bildung*: I become someone because of what I have been through, what I have endured in losing and gaining, in remembering and forgetting, in venture and return.

Thank the gods, too, that he was able to admit out loud that "every experience worthy of the name" (p. 356) involves suffering. It involves opening ourselves to the open-ended sojourn of things, their ongoingness and fragilities and sometimes exhilarating, sometimes terrifying possibilities and fluidities (interpretation "makes the object and all its possibilities fluid" [p. 367]) . This is central to the arguments in his *Truth and Method*: that experience (*Erfahrung*) is not something we *have*: it is something we *undergo*, and, to put it more intergenerationally, something we just might *endure*. It therefore has to do with duration, with what lasts, and therefore with what can be cultivated, taken care of: experiences worthy of the name are not interior mental events had by a self-same subject, but are more like places that hold memory, topographical endurances (like these riveredges) full of ancestry and mystery and a complex, unrepayable indebtedness. Full of dependencies, full of "it depends," full of dependents. And more, experience therefore links with my own endurance, what I can live with, which, in part, means where I need to be, in what "space," (in what relations) to endure.

That, of course, is why these last months have been so humiliating coupled as they have been with a forgetting of what I need to endure. The question seems to be, again, how could I have forgotten this, again?

It may be, however, that such earthbound forgetting is inevitable, as may be having to endure such forgetting again and again.

This gives human experience the character of a journeying (another meaning buried in *Erfahrung*), becoming someone along the way, but never in such a way that suffering is simply overcome or finished, but only in such a way that, perhaps even for a moment, the stranglehold of consciousness may be gracefully interrupted by the dusty world and the unanticipated plop and peep of an American Dipper off a midriver rock.

So here's the rub. Forgetting these things that sustain me is akin to Martin Heidegger's terrible idea, cited in the long passage above, that we can somehow sometimes do the impossible. Human will—our "wanting and doing" (Gadamer, 1989, p. xxviii)—with all its consequent unearthly Cartesian dreams of an earth full of isolated substances, isolated "objects" bereft of relations, can push us beyond the allotted sphere of the fleshy, earthy relations we need to sustain us, into doing things that overstep the allotted sphere of the possible and are thus impossible.

We can, that is, work against the conditions under which our work might be actually accomplishable.

I can, like this darkening winter mood, "not be myself."

And even though I may then still be on earth, I can act out of a forgetting of this given, this gift, worldless mumbling a soft cocoon of merely words that have lost their sensuous spells, their fleshy referents, their hum and rattle on the breath.

III

All things show faces, the world not only a coded signature to be read for meaning, but a physiognomy to be faced. As expressive forms, things speak; they show the shape they are in. They announce themselves, bear witness to their presence: "Look, here we are." They regard us beyond how we may regard them, our perspectives, what we intend with them, and how we dispose of them. (Hillman, 1982, p. 77)

So what of those odd things we often surround our children with in schools? Odd objects that have lost their body, their richness, their rigor, their recursiveness, their relations (Doll, 1993)? Objects that seem to have no ancestors, no place, no *topos*, no topographies, no lives, objects that might be memorizable but not memorable, that don't bear remembering, that don't require our suffering the journey of coming to understand them and therefore coming to understand ourselves differently having understood them?

What witness do such things bear on us and our doings? Not "what do we have to say about them" but "what do they have to say about us."

(Spotted!)

Many of the things our children are surrounded with in school are simply isolated activities (simply our own "wanting[s] and doing[s]" (Gadamer, 1989, p. xxviii) instead of places to go full of their own wantings and doings, places to inhabit, places to take care of and cultivate, places the travelling of which might require us to become someone in the presence of others who travel with us and in the presence of this place which itself will shape our character (Jardine, 1997a).

Many of the things we all surround ourselves with are unable to show their suffering, their care, their relations, their topographies.

Consider this Styrofoam cup I'm just about to throw away. It is produced as part of a standing reserve (Heidegger, 1977) for something else (just like math facts are produced as part of a standing reserve for the accumulation of marks and grades). It (and from here on, we're speaking of the Styrofoam cup but also imagining at the same time the frantic little do-its of mad math minutes) is so disposable (so without position or place, without composure, one might say), that any relations of it or to it cannot be cultivated, chosen, cared for, remembered, enjoyed, either by us or anything else that surrounds it. I cannot become composed around such a thing. There will be no mourning at its loss or destruction. It does not show its having-arrived-here and we have no need to try to remember such an arrival. All trace of relations and endurance are gone. In fact, it does not endure. It does not age.

It breaks.

In fact, it is produced deliberately in order to *not* hold attention, *not* take on character, *not* arouse any sense or possibility of care or concern. *It is deliberately produced in order to not be remembered* . It is deliberately produced of forgetting. It is *Lethe*. It is lethal.

It is what we use so that our ability to remember the care and suffering that constitutes the interdependencies of the earth (and therewith the possibility of remembering our own suffering) is not visible and seems to be not necessary. But worse, *it "is" in such a way that care is not even possible.*

It is impossible.

And, to the extent that our human life and this great earth life is constituted by the attentiveness and suffering of all its relations (Heidegger's [1962] understanding of care as *Sorge* and his insistence, along with Gadamer's [1989], on our "finitude"), to that extent, this Styrofoam cup is impossible, even though *there it is.*

So the problem with such things—and therefore the problem with surrounding ourselves and our children with such things—is their impossibility. Human will has produced something that has spiraled out of the order of relations. The problem with the disposability of this cup is not simply the products or by-products of its manufacture or the non-biodegradability of what remains of it after its use (this is ecologically consciousness at its most literal minded). The deep ecological problem with it is that it is unable to be cared for, and living in its presence therefore weakens, undermines, or occludes our ability to see how our lives and this earth are constituted by such suffering. And, too, the problem with the disposability of isolated math facts is that they are unable to be cared for and living in their presence therefore weakens, undermines, or occludes our ability to see how we might understand mathematics as a living place, a living inheritance with which we have been entrusted, full of its own hidden agencies that live "beyond my wanting and doing." [Gadamer, 1989, p. xxviii], and therefore that can, potentially, release me from my [schooled] isolation out into a *world* of relations.

This Styrofoam cup becomes a perfect example of a Cartesian substance: something that is bereft of any relations. This Styrofoam cup thus stands there in the world "by itself," as an object produced of bereaving. But it also promises to help us get over our sense of loss through a relentless, ever accelerating stream of consumptiveness: one faceless, bodiless, placeless, careless cup after the other—just like one faceless, bodiless, placeless, careless schooly math activity after the other—all bent to the satisfaction of our "wanting and doing."

And then, of course, we excuse the existence of such cups by pointing to our own convenience, never once suspecting that our sense of convenience has been manufactured by and is now housed in the very cups that use our sense of convenience as their excuse. And, just as evidently, we inundate our children with relentless streams of one activity after the other and excuse it by referring to their "short attention spans," never once suspecting that

many of the things they are inundated with in schools *are
not worthy of attention*, because they have been stripped of
their imaginal topographies (their living "ecologies," we
might say). We thus become caught in producing rushed,
impossible activities to service the very attentions we have
violated through such production. A *perfect* image of
knowledge-as-consumption-and-production, knowledge as
a scarce resource, and school as commodified exchange
processes bent on producing consumers in a forgetfulness
of the original given, the original gift (Jardine, Clifford, &
Friesen, in press; what Matthew Fox [1990] called "the
original blessing" [p. 23] of the earth). Since, in such an
economy of consumption, "time [itself] is always running
out" (Berry, 1987, p. 44), the only hope, in the midst of
such a rush of activities is not slowing down and opening
up rich fields of relations. Rather, hope is found only in
accelerating the rush [Jardine, 1995, 1996, 1997] in a grand
eschatological race for the End Times: a time when wholeness will be achieved once all the scattered bits and pieces
of the curriculum are finally "covered." These impossible,
consumptive, isolated, never really satisfying bits and pieces
thus always leave us looking longingly for the last days
when all will be redeemed and we can finally rest, assured.
Differently put, our relentless consumptivism is premised
on a desire for it to end in the full satisfaction guaranteed
of our "wanting and doing."

IV

In the summer of 1998 I taught a course on hermeneutics at the University of Victoria, and we spent our last
class considering James Hillman's *"Anima Mundi*: Return-

ing the Soul to the World" (1982). There is a certain point in this essay where the image of an object cut off from all its relations is brought up, an object unable to return to the gods that made it, an object unplaced. In our class, I offered up the image of a fragment of Styrofoam cup buried ten feet underground in some long-forgotten dumpsite.

Darkwormyness. The roiling relief of decays, where all things begin to return to the gods that made them, begin to empty out from their illusion of self-containment into all their relations. And then, right in the midst of these rich, dark, moist underworlds, these rich sufferings, this dry brightlit brightwhite self-contained, "clear and distinct" (Descartes, 1955), full present, unreposing, Utopian thing, unable to let go of its self, unable to find its lost relations (excuse the Heideggerianism, but unable to *world*).

Oddly impossible, having overstepped something unutterable, now condemned, it seems, to never re-turn, never to con-verse, never to breath out into its topography..

Hillman says that this image of an object that has "no way back to the gods" (p. 83) is precisely an image of a "figure in Hell" (p. 83).

V

In *Truth and Method* (1989), Hans-Georg Gadamer insists that "youth [and, of necessity, anyone new to anything] demands images for its imagination and for the forming of its memory. [We must, therefore] supplement the *critica* of Cartesianism with the old *topica*." (p. 21). The "*critica* of Cartesianism" are essentially methodological and procedural. As Martin Heidegger (1972, 66) has noted, in this fulfillment of the modern age, "the matters at hand become matters of method." Once this Cartesian inheritance is enacted in schools, isolated, anonymous, disembodied, clear and distinct, methodologically reproducible and assessable math facts become understood as more "basic" than the troublesome, roiling, ongoing, irreproducible, ambiguous, highly personally and bodily engaging conversations we might have with children and colleagues about living mathematical relations. Ideologically, under the hood of Cartesianism, such living conversations blur and despoil and contaminate and desecrate what is in fact objective and certain and self-contained.

"We are living out a logic [of fragmentation and isolation] that is centuries old and that is being worked out in our own lifetime" (Berman, 1983, p. 23). Against this modernist logic, Gadamer insists that understanding and its memorial formation require the productive supplementation of topographical imagination, thus placing what might have seemed to be isolated "math facts" back into the sustaining relations that make them what they are, that keep them sane, that make them rich and memorable. "The old *topica*" is thus essentially not methodological but substantial, full of smells and names and faces and kin, full of ancestral roots and ongoing conversations and old wisdoms and new, fresh deliberateness and audacity and life. It is also necessarily and unavoidably multifarious, contentious, ongoing, intergenerational, and unable to be foreclosed with any certainty because, for example, as a *living* discipline, mathematics endures. Therefore, topographically-hermeneutically-ecologically, "understanding mathematics" means going to this living place and getting in on the living conversation that constitutes its being furthered.

Understanding is thus not method: it is *learning to dwelling in the presence of this riveredge, or learning to dwell in the presence of Pythagorean proportionality* and, under such witness, becoming someone because of it.

VI

> As unhidden, truth has in itself an inner tension and ambiguity. Being contains something like a hostility to its own presentations. The existing thing does not simply offer us a recognizable and familiar surface contour; it also has an inner depth of self-sufficiency that Heidegger calls "standing-in-itself." The complete unhiddenness of all beings, their total objectification (by means of a representation that conceives things in their perfect state) would negate this standing-in-itself of beings and lead to a total leveling of them. A complete objectification of this kin would no longer represent beings that stand in their own being. Rather, it would represent nothing more than our opportunity for using beings, and what would be manifest would be the will that seizes upon and dominates things. [By this riveredge] we experience an absolute opposition to this will-to-control, not in the sense of a rigid resistance to the presumption of our will, which is bent on utilizing things, but in the sense of the superior and intrusive power of a being reposing in itself. (Gadamer, 1977, p. 226-7)

The project of hermeneutics requires that we strive to "overcome the epistemological problem" (Gadamer, 1989, pp. 242-264). The healing art of interpretation is not concerned, simply with knowing things differently than Cartesianism allows. Rather, it requires that we strive to "break open the *being* of the object" (p. 362) we are considering. Things, taken up interpretively, *exist differently* than the logic of self-containedness and self-identity allows. The healing art of interpretation is thus first and foremost *ontological* in its movement.

Living things in this world *are* all their vast, ancestral, intergenerational, earthly relations. *This* is the greatness and power of their "repose." They *are* all the ways, all the voices, that have handed them to us, a great and vast receding spaciousness, where "beings hold themselves back by coming forward into the openness of presence" (Gadamer, 1977, p. 227). This riveredge *is* all its relations sounding outwards into all things and back and forth in the cascades of generational voices faded and to come. It isn't first some thing and somehow "then" in relation (which gives rise to "the epistemological problem"). "Only *in* the multifariousness of such voices does it exist." (Gadamer, 1989, p. 284). And it resists objectification—it "holds itself back" in repose—because it is unfinished. It is open to the endurances and sufferings to come which can never be fully or finally "given." "The whole" is never given (Gadamer, 1989, p. 38) and its therefore never fully present or presentable or representable (this is the great "critique of presence" that Heidegger initiated as a critique of the Being of things, not an epistemological critique).

And, if the whole is never simply given, health is never given. Healing and wounding, like memory and forgetting, like *sol stasis* and return, are never done. Again, suffering, endurance, furtherance:

> This ultimately forces an awareness that even [a simple thing like a twirl of dust kicked up from the path, or a seemingly isolated math fact, or the seemingly pristine givenness of Pythagorean theorem] possesses its own

original worldliness and, thus, the center of its own Being so long as it is not placed in the object-world of producing and marketing. Our orientation to [such things, unlike our orientation to the object-world] is always something like our orientation to an inheritance. (Gadamer, 1994, pp. 191-2)

The act of understanding such things is not a matter of utilizing or controling or making fully present and objective or making completely clear. It is the act of participating in the work of "handing down" (Gadamer, 1989, p. 284) such things. However, we must also cultivate in ourselves the ability and the desire to adamantly *refuse* (Jardine, 1994) some inheritances, those that toy with impossibility and despoil our ability to dwell in the suffering of things (that despoil our ability to *experience* [*Erfahrung*]). We must refuse the leveling that violates the deeply ecopedagogical repose of things.

So even when a young child simply counts up to ten, to *understand* such an event means to allow ourselves to experience (*Erfahrung*) how they are standing with us in the middle of a great human inheritance, a great human endurance, full of arcs of ancestry and memory that define mathematics as a living discipline. This is one of us, one of our kind, one of our kin, counting out in an act that is of a kind with the measured pacing of birdcalls heralding the sun's arcing higher and higher.

Under such an image of our work as educators, the task of learning the ways of a place like mathematics becomes akin to the task of becoming native to a place, developing

...the sense of "nativeness," of belonging to the place [see the detail with which Gadamer (1989, p. 462) deals with the idea of understanding-as-belonging and the relationship between belonging (Zugehorigkeit) and hearing (Horen)]. Some people are beginning to try to understand where they are, and what it would means to live carefully and wisely, delicately in a place, in such a way that you can live there adequately and comfortably. Also, your children and grandchildren and generations a thousand years in the future will still be able to live there. That's thinking as though you were a native. Thinking in terms of the whole fabric of living and life. (Snyder, 1980, p. 86)

Thus it is that there is a great kinship between hermeneutics, ecology, and pedagogy. They are each, in their own ways, concerned with returning us to our suffering and to the suffering we must undergo to understand our place in this great earthly inheritance, full as it is with both riveredges and the graceful beauty of Pythagoras—these two now no longer different in kind, both understood as finally able to return to the gods that made them.

Endbit

"Understanding is an adventure and, like any adventure, it always involves some risk." (Gadamer, 1983, p. 141). In fact, *"understanding proves to be,"* not a method but an *"event"* (Gadamer, 1989, p. 308), a moment of the fluttering open of the meticulous co-arisings that repose around any thing.

This is what hermeneutics understands as "truth": *Alethia*, the opening of what was previously closed (and therefore, like the necessary dialectic of memory and forgetting, the necessary closing off of things as well, part of the "hostility towards full presentation" that Gadamer has alluded to), the remembering of what was forgotten (*Lethe* as the river of forgetfulness and our living in the wisdom that "only by forgetting does the mind have the possibility of seeing things with fresh eyes, so that what is familiar fuses with the new. 'Keeping in mind' is [thus] ambiguous" [Gadamer, 1989, p. 16]), the making alive, the livening up, of what was dull and leveled and therefore deadly (lethal) and morose.

As for me, I'll sit here a bit, near solstice, facing Sol's perennial highpitched summer stasis over the Tropic of Capricorn.

Sun's re-turning (*tropos*) in the sign of the Goat.

Undergoing, with fresh eyes, my own "slower, more miraculous returns" (Wallace, 1987) to the gods that made me.

CHAPTER Seventeen

ALL BEINGS ARE YOUR ANCESTORS

A Bear Sutra on Ecology, Buddhism, and Pedagogy

Transforming according to circumstances, meet all beings as your ancestors. (Hongzhi Zhengjue [1091-1157])

I

JUST SPOTTED A YEAR-OLD black bear crossing HWY. 66 @ McLean Creek, heading north.

From a distance, struggling at first to resolve its color and lowness and lopey canter into dog or cat likenesses as it stretched up to the side of the road and across and suddenly slowed into distinctive roundhumpness...bear!

Stopped and watched him amble up the shalysteep creekedge. Wet. Greenglistening. Breath arriving plumey

225

in the damp and cold after days of heat waves...been 33
degrees C. and more for four days running in the foothills
of the Rockies west of Calgary. Here, roaming in the edge
between prairie and forest, between flatlands and hills and
mountains—here, when summers break, they tend to break
deeply.

Cold rain. Cold.

It is so thrilling to not be accustomed to this sort of
experience, to have it still be so *pleasurable*. Bear. His presence almost unbelievable, making this whole place waver
and tremble, making my assumptions and presumptions
and thoughts and tales of experiences in this place suddenly wonderfully irrelevant and so much easier to write
because of such irrelevance.

Bear's making this whole place show its fragility and
momentariness and serendipities.

Bear's making my own fragility and momentariness
show.

That is what is most shocking. This unforeseeable happenstance of bear's arrival and my own happiness are oddly
linked. This "hap" (Weinsheimer, 1987, pp. 7-8) hovering
at the heart of the world.

My own life as serendipitous, despite my earnest plans.
Giddy sensation, this.

Like little bellybreath tingles on downarcing childgiggle
swingsets.

Felt in the *tanden* (Sekida, 1975, pp. 18-9, 66-67) in
Walking Meditation (Nhat Hanh, 1995).

Breath's gutty basement. Nearby, the lowest Chakra
tingles with an upspine burst to whitesparkle brilliance
just overhead and out in front of the forehead.

In moments like this, something flutters *open*. Shifting
fields of relations bloom. Wind stirs nothing. Not just my

alertness and sudden attention, but the odd sensation of knowing that these trees, this creek, this bear, are all *already* alert to me in ways proper to each and despite my attention. Something flutters *open*, beyond this centered self.

With the presence of this ambly bear, the whole of things arrives, fluttered open.

II

All Beings are your Ancestors. The feary sight of him, teaching me, reminding me of forgotten shared ancestries, forgotten shared relations to earth and air and fire and water.

That strange little lesson having to be learned again: that he has been here all along, cleaving this shared ancestry, cleaving this shared earth of ours, making and forming my life beyond my "wanting and doing," (Gadamer, 1989, p. xxviii), beyond my wakefulness and beyond my remembering.

It is not so much that this bear is an "other" (Shepard, 1996), but that it is a *relative*, that is most deeply transformative and alarming to my ecological somnambulance and forgetfulness. It is not just that I might come awake and start to remember these deep, earthy relations.

It is also that, even if I don't, they all still bear witness to my life.

Relations. Who would have thought? Coming across *one of us* that I had forgotten.

Coming, therefore, across myself *as also one of us*. Such a funny thing to be surprised about again. In the face of this Great Alert Being, I, again, become one of us!

Great Alert Being, this bear. Great Teacher. His and my meaty bodies both of the same "flesh of the [earth]" (Abram, 1996, pp. 66-67), rapt in silent conversations (p. 49).

Where, my god, have I been? And what have I been saying, betraying of myself and my distraction?

III

This bear ambles in the middle of all its earthly relations to wind and sky and rain and berries and roadsides and the eons of beings that helped hone that creek edge to just those small pebbly falls under the weight of his paws:

> Even the very tiniest thing, to the extent that it "is," displays in its act of being the whole web of circuminsessional interpenetration that links all things together. (Nishitani, 1982, p. 150)

The whole earth conspires to make just these simple events just exactly like this:

"Within each dust mote is vast abundance." (Hongzhi, 1991, p. 14) This is the odd butterfly effect (Glieck, 1987, p. 17) fluttering in the stomach.

This, too, is the profound co-implication of all beings that is part of ecological mindfulness—that each being is implicated in the whole of things and, if we are able to experience it from the belly, from each being a deep relatedness to all beings can be unfolded, can be understood, can be felt, can be adored, can be praised in prayerful grace, a giving thanks (Snyder, 1990, pp. 175-185). Lovely intermingling of thinking and thanksgiving (Heidegger, 1968).

So the thrill of seeing this bear is, in part, the exhilarating rush felt in seeing it explode outwards, emptying itself into all its relations, and then retracting to just that black bear, now an exquisite still-spot ambling at the center of all things. And more!

> The center is everywhere. Each and every thing becomes the center of all things and, in that sense, becomes an absolute center. This is the absolute uniqueness of things, their reality. (Nishitani, 1982, p. 146)

Like breath exhaled outwards and then drawn in deep draughts. This inwardness and outwardness of emptiness (Sanskrit: *sunyata*; Japanese: *ku*)—each thing *is* its relatedness to all things, reflecting each in each in Indra's Netted Jewels, and yet each thing is always just itself, irreplaceable. Smells of the forests of mid-August and the sweetness of late summer wild flowers. Winey bloomy blush. Intoxicating.

All Beings are your Ancestors.

IV

Hey, bear!

If we are to meet all beings as our ancestors, we must also meet all those very same beings as our descendants. This odd, fluid, difficult, shifting edge point between the ancestors and the descendants is where our humanity lives.

This is "the empty field" (Hongzhi, 1991) that opens and embraces.

It is also the lifespot of teaching and learning and transmission and transformation.

There are many Great Teachers.
All praise to bear and his subtle gift.

—*Bragg Creek, Alberta, August 8-10, 1997*

REFERENCES

Abram, D. (1996). *The Spell of the Sensuous: Language in a More-Than-Human World*. New York: Pantheon Books.

Arendt, H. (1969). *Between Past and Future*. London: Penguin Books.

Berlin, J. (1988). "Rhetoric and Ideology in the Writing Class," *College English*, 50(5): pp. 477-494.

Berman, M. (1983). *The Reenchantment of the World*. New York: Bantam Books.

Berry, W. (1977). *The Unsettling of America*. San Francisco: Sierra Club Books.

Berry, W. (1983). *Standing by Words*. San Francisco: North Point Press.

Berry, W. (1987). *Home Economics*. San Francisco: North Point Press.

Berry, W. (1988). "The Profit in Work's Pleasure," *Harper's Magazine*, March, 1989, pp. 19-24.

Bordo, S. (1988). *The Flight to Objectivity*. Albany: State University of New York Press.

Calkins, L.M. (1986). *The Art of Teaching Writing*. Portsmouth, NH: Heinemann.

Caputo, J. (1987). *Radical Hermeneutics*. Bloomington: Indiana State University Press.

Caputo, J. (1989). *Against Ethics: Contributions to a Poetics of Obligation with Constant Reference to Deconstruction*. Bloomington: Indiana State University Press.

Chua-Eoan, H. (1991). "The Uses of Monsters," *Time*. August 12, 1991, p. 27.

Clifford, J. (1986). "On Ethnographic Allegory," in Clifford, J. & Marcus, G. (eds.) (1986). *Writing Culture: The Poetics and Poli-*

tics of Ethnography. Berkeley: University of California Press, pp. 98-121.

Clifford, P. & Friesen, S. (1993). "A Curious Plan: Managing on the Twelfth," *Harvard Educational Review*, 63(3), pp. 339-358.

Clifford, P. & Friesen, S. (1994). "Choosing to Be Healers," *JCT Conference on Curriculum Theory and Classroom Practice.* Banff, Alberta, October.

Clifford, P. & Friesen, S. (1995). "Transgressive Energy: The Necessary Delinquency of Pandora, Eve and Willful Children," *JCT Conference on Curriculum Theory and Classroom Practice*, Chattanooga TN, September-October, 1995.

Clifford, P., Friesen, S., & Jardine, D. (1995). "Reading Coyote Reading the World: Meditations on Whole Language, Edgy Literacy and the Work of the World," *National Reading Conference*, New Orleans, December, 1995.

Descartes, R. (1955). *Descartes Selections.* New York: Scribners.

Devall, G. & Sessions, B. (1985). *Deep Ecology.* Salt Lake City: Peregrine Books.

Doll, W. (1993). "Curriculum Possibilities in a 'Post'-Future," *Journal of Curriculum and Supervision* , 8(4), pp. 277-292.

Edelsky, C., Altwerger, B., & Flores, B. (1991). *Whole Language: What's the Difference?* Portsmouth, NH: Heinemann.

Eliade, M. (1968). *Myth and Reality.* New York: Harper and Row.

Fischer, M. (1986). "Ethnicity and the Post-Modern Arts of Memory," in Clifford, J. & Marcus, G. (eds.) (1986). *Writing Culture: The Poetics and Politics of Ethnography.* Berkeley: University of California Press.

Fowler, H. & Fowler, F. (eds.) (1964). *The Concise Oxford Dictionary of Current English.* Oxford: Clarendon Press.

Fox, M. (1983). *Original Blessing.* Santa Fe: Bear and Co.

Friesen, S., Clifford, P., & Jardine, D. (1998). "On the Intergenerational Character of Mathematical Truth," *JCT: An Interdisciplinary Journal of Curriculum Studies.*

Gadamer, H.G. (1977). *Philosophical Hermeneutics.* Berkeley: University of California Press.

Gadamer, H.G. (1983). *Reason in the Age of Science.* Cambridge, MA: MIT Press.

Gadamer, H.G. (1989). *Truth and Method*, second revised edition. New York: Crossroad Books.

Gadamer, H.G. (1994). *Heidegger's Ways*. Boston: MIT Press

Gadamer, H.G. (1983). *Reason in the Age of Science*. Boston: MIT Press.

Gadamer, H.G. (1996a). "Apologia for the Art of Healing," in Gadamer, H.G. (1996). *The Enigma of Health*. Stanford, CA: Stanford University Press.

Gadamer, H.G. (1996b). "On the Enigmatic Character of Health," in Gadamer, H.G., *The Enigma of Health*. Stanford, CA: Stanford University Press.

Gadamer, H.G. (1996c). "The Experience of Death," in Gadamer, H.G., *The Enigma of Health*. Stanford, CA: Stanford University Press.

Glieck, J. (1987). *Chaos: The Making of a New Science*. New York: Penguin Books.

Graves, D.H. (1983). *Writing: Teachers and Children at Work*. Portsmouth, NH: Heinemann.

Habermas, J. (1973). *Knowledge and Human Interests*. Boston: Beacon Books.

Hanh, N. (1985). *A Guide to Walking Meditation*. New Haven: Eastern Press Inc.

Harste, J.C., Short, K.G., & Burke, C. (1988). *Creating Classrooms for Authors: The Reading-Writing Connection*. Portsmouth, NH: Heinemann.

Heidegger, M. (1947). "Letter on Humanism," in Heidegger, M. (1977). *Basic Writings*. New York: Harper and Row.

Heidegger, M. (1962). *Being and Time*. New York: Harper and Row.

Heidegger, M. (1972). *Time and Being*. New York: Harper and Row.

Heidegger, M. (1977). "The Question Concerning Technology," in Heidegger, M. (1977). *Basic Writings*. New York: Harper and Row.

Heidegger, M. (1968). *What is Called Thinking?* New York: Harper and Row.

Heidegger, M. (1977). "The Age of the World-Picture," in *The Question Concerning Technology*. New York: Harper & Row, pp. 115-154.

Heidegger, M. (1985). *History of the Concept of Time.* Bloomington: Indiana University Press.

Heidegger, M. (1987). "Overcoming Metaphysics," in *The End of Philosophy.* New York: Harper and Row.

Hillman, J. (1975). "Abandoning the Child," in Hillman, J. (1975). *Loose Ends.* Dallas: Spring Publications.

Hillman, J. (1982). "*Anima Mundi*: Returning the Soul to the World," *Spring.* Vol. 40.

Hillman, J. (1987). *Puer Papers.* Dallas: Spring Publications.

Hillman, J. (1989). *Healing Fiction.* Barrytown: Station Hill Press.

Hillman, J. (1991). *Inter Views.* Dallas: Spring Publications.

Hongzhi. Z. (1991). *Cultivating the Empty Field: The Silent Illumination of Zen Master Hongzhi.* Leighton, T.D. & Wu, Y. (trans.). San Francisco: North Point Press.

Husserl, E. (1970). *The Crisis of European Science and Transcendental Phenomenology.* Evanston: Northwestern University Press.

Ignatow, D. (1980). [Untitled], in Bly, R. (ed.) (1980). *News of the Universe: Poems of Twofold Consciousness.* San Francisco: Sierra Club Books, p. 123.

Jardine, D.W. (1988). "There Are Children All Around Us," *Journal of Educational Thought,* 22(2A), pp. 178-186.

Jardine, D.W. (1990). "'To Dwell with a Boundless Heart': On the Integrated Curriculum and the Recovery of the Earth," *Journal of Curriculum and Supervision.* 5(2), pp. 107-119, reprinted in Jardine (1998).

Jardine, D.W. (1990a). "On the Humility of Mathematical Language," *Educational Theory.* 40(2), pp. 181-192, reprinted in Jardine (1998).

Jardine, D.W. (1990b). "Awakening from Descartes' Nightmare: On the Love of Ambiguity in Phenomenological Approaches to Education," *Studies in Philosophy and Education,* 10(1).

Jardine, D.W. (1992). "'The Fecundity of the Individual Case': Considerations of the Pedagogic Heart of Interpretive Work," *Journal of Philosophy of Education.* 26(1), pp. 51-61.

Jardine, D.W. (1992a). *Speaking with a Boneless Tongue.* Bragg Creek: Makyo Press.

Jardine, D.W. (1992b). "The Pedagogic Wound and the Pathologies of Doubt," in Levering, B., Van Manen, M., & Miedema, S. (eds.). *Reflections on Pedagogy and Method, Vol. II.* Montfoort, Netherlands: Uriah Heep, pp. 97-112.

Jardine, D.W. (1992c). "Immanuel Kant, Jean Piaget and the Rage for Order: Hints of the Colonial Spirit in Pedagogy," *Educational Philosophy and Theory.* 23(1), pp. 28-43, reprinted in Jardine (1998).

Jardine, D.W. (1992d). "Reflections on Hermeneutics, Education and Ambiguity: Hermeneutics As a Restoring of Life to Its Original Difficulty," in Pinar, W. & Reynolds, W. (eds.). *Understanding Curriculum as Phenomenological and Deconstructed Text.* New York: Teacher's College Press.

Jardine, D.W. (1994). "'Littered with Literacy': An Ecopedagogical Reflection on Whole Language, Pedocentrism and the Necessity of Refusal," *Journal of Curriculum Studies.* 26(5), pp. 509-524.

Jardine, D.W. (1994). "Student-Teaching, Interpretation and the Monstrous Child," *Journal of Philosophy of Education.* 28(1), pp. 17-24.

Jardine, D.W. (1995). "The Stubborn Particulars of Grace," in Horwood, B. (ed.). *Experience and the Curriculum: Principles and Programs.* Dubuque, IA: Kendall/Hunt Publishing Company, pp. 261-275.

Jardine, D.W. (1995a). "'Because It Shows Us the Way at Night': On Animism, Interpretive Writing and the Reanimation of Piagetian Theory," *JCT Conference on Curriculum Theory and Classroom Practice.* Chattanooga, TN, September-October 1995.

Jardine, D.W. (1996/1997). "'Under the Tough Old Stars': Pedagogical Hyperactivity and the Mood of Environmental Education," *Canadian Journal of Environmental Education,* 1(spring, 1996), 48-55, reprinted in *Clearing: Environmental Education in the Pacific Northwest.* No. 97, April-May, 1997, pp. 20-23.

Jardine, D.W. (1996). "The Profession Needs New Blood," *JCT: An Interdisciplinary Journal of Curriculum Studies,* pp. 105-130.

Jardine, D.W. (1997) "'All Beings Are Your Ancestors': A Bear Sutra on Ecology, Buddhism and Pedagogy," *The Trumpeter: A Journal of Ecosophy.* 14(3), pp. 122-23.

Jardine, D.W. (1997a). "The Surroundings," *JCT: The Journal of Cur-*

riculum Theorizing, 13(3), pp. 18-21.

Jardine, D.W. (1998). *"To Dwell with a Boundless Heart": On Curriculum Theory, Hermeneutics and the Ecological Imagination.* New York: Peter Lang Publishers.

Jardine, D.W. & Field, J. (1992). "'Disproportion, Monstrousness and Mystery': Ecological and Ethical Reflections on the Initiation of Student-Teachers into the Community of Education," *Teaching and Teacher Education*, 8(1), pp. 301-310.

Jardine, D.W. with Friesen, S. (1997). "A Play on the Wickedness of Undone Sums, Including a Brief Mytho-Phenomenology of 'x' and Some Speculations on the Effects of Its Peculiar Absence in Elementary Mathematics Education," *Journal of the Philosophy of Mathematics Education*. 10.

Jardine, D.W., Clifford, P., & Friesen, S. (in press). "Globalization and the Pedagogical Prospects of the Gift," *Alberta Journal of Educational Research*.

Jardine, D.W. & Misgeld, D. (1989) "Hermeneutics As the Undisciplined Child," in Packer, M. & Addison, R. (eds.). *Entering the Circle: Hermeneutic Investigations in Psychology*. Albany: State University of New York Press.

Johnson, T. (1990). "Announcing...These Dynamite Workshops to Help You on the Road to Becoming a Whole Language Pro" (advertisement), *Reading Today*, 8(1), p. 32.

Kant, I. (1767/1964). *Critique of Pure Reason*. London: MacMillan.

Kundera, M. (1990). *Immortality*. New York: HarperCollins.

Le Guin, U.K. (1968). *A Wizard of Earthsea*. New York: Penguin.

Merleau-Ponty, M. (1964). *The Phenomenology of Perception*. London: Routledge.

Merleau-Ponty, M. (1968). *The Visible and the Invisible*. Evanston: Northwestern University Press.

Merleau-Ponty, M. (1972). "Everywhere and Nowhere," *Signs*. Evanston: Northwestern University Press.

Meschonnic, H. (1988). "Rhyme and Life," *Critical Inquiry*, 15, Autumn.

Miller, A. (1989). *For Your Own Good: Hidden Cruelty in Child-Rearing and the Roots of Violence*. Toronto: Collins.

Misgeld, D., Jardine, D.W., & Grahame, P. (1985). "Communicative

Competence, Practical Reasoning, and the Understanding of Culture," *Phenomenology + Pedagogy*, 3(3).

Misgeld, D. & Jardine, D.W. (1989). "Hermeneutics As the Undisciplined Child: Hermeneutic and Technical Images of Education," in Parker, M. & Addison, R. (eds.). *Entering the Circle: Hermeneutic Inquiry in Psychology*. Albany: State University of New York Press, pp. 259-274.

Neufeldt, V. & Guralnik, D.B. (1988). *Webster's New World Dictionary of American English: Third College Edition*. New York: Simon & Schuster

Newman, J.M. (1985). *Whole Language: Theory in Use*. Portsmouth, NH: Heinemann.

Nhat H.(1986). *The Miracle of Mindfulness*. Berkeley: Parallax Press.

Nhat, H. (1995). *The Long Road Turns to Joy: A Guide to Walking Meditation*. Berkeley: Parallax Press.

Nishitani, K. (1982). *Religion and Nothingness*. Berkeley: University of California Press.

Palmer, P. (1989). *To Know As We Are Known: Education As a Spiritual Discipline*. New York: HarperCollins.

Peterson, R.T. (1980). *A Field Guide to the Birds East of the Rockies*. 4th Edition. Boston: Houghton Mifflin.

Piaget, J. (1952). *Origins of Intelligence in Children*. New York: International Universities Press.

Piaget, J. (1965). *Insights and Illusions of Philosophy*. New York: Meridian Books.

Piaget, J. (1968). *Structuralism*. New York: Harper and Row.

Piaget, J. (1973). *Psychology of Intelligence*. Totowa, NJ: Littlefield, Adams.

Piaget, J. (1974). *The Construction of Reality in the Child*. New York: Ballantine Books.

Piaget, J. & Inhelder, B. (1972). *The Child's Construction of Quantities*. London: Routledge & Kegan Paul.

Ricoeur, P. (1980). Cited in Kermode, F. *The Genesis of Secrecy: On the Interpretation of Narrative*. Cambridge, MA: Harvard University Press, p. 80.

Shepard, P. (1996). *The Others: How Animals Made Us Human*. Washington, DC: Island Press.

Shirane, H. (1996). *Traces of Dreams: Landscape, Cultural Memory and the Poetry of Basho*. Stanford: Stanford University Press.

Smith, D. (1986). "Brighter Than a Thousand Suns: Facing Pedagogy in the Nuclear Shadow," presented at the Fifth Triennial World Conference on Education, Hiroshima, Japan, July-August, 1986, reprinted in Smith (1999).

Smith, D. (1988). "Children and the Gods of War," *Journal of Educational Thought*, 22A (2).

Smith, D. (1988b). "On Being Critical About Language: The Critical Theory Tradition and Implications for Language Education," *Reading-Canada-Lecture*, 6(4), pp. 243-248.

Smith, D. (1988c). *From Logocentrism to Rhysomatics: Breaking Through the Boundary Police to a New Love*," presented at the Bergamo Conference on Curriculum Theory and Classroom Practice, Dayton, OH.

Smith, D. (1991). "Hermeneutic Inquiry: The Hermeneutic Imagination and the Pedagogic Text," in Short, E. (ed.). *Forms of Curriculum Inquiry*. New York: State University of New York Press.

Smith, D. (1999). *Pedagon: Interdisciplinary Essays in the Human Sciences, Pedagogy and Culture*. New York: Peter Lang Publishers.

Snyder, G. (1980). *The Real Work*. New York: New Directions Books.

Spangler, D. & Thompson, W. (1991). *Re-Imagination of the World: A Critique of the New Age, Science and Popular Culture*. Santa Fe: Bear.

Trungpa, C. (1990). *Cutting Through Spiritual Materialism*. San Francisco: Shambhala Press.

Turner, V. (1987). "Betwixt and Between: The Liminal Period in Rites of Passage," in Foster, S., Little, M., & Mahdi, L.C. *Betwixt and Between: Patterns of Masculine and Feminine Initiation*. LaSalle, IL: Open Court, pp. 3-22.

Usher, R. & Edwards, R. (1994). *Postmodernism and Education*. London: Routledge.

Wallace, B. (1987). *The Stubborn Particulars of Grace*. Toronto: McClelland and Stewart.

Weaver, C. (1990). *Understanding Whole Language: From Principles to Practice*. Portsmouth, NH: Heinemann.

Weinsheimer, J. (1987). *Gadamer's Hermeneutics*. New Haven: Yale University Press.

Wilde, S. (1996). *Awakening Care: A Possibility at the Heart of Teaching*, unpublished Master's thesis, Faculty of Education, University of Calgary.

Williams, W.C. (1991). "Spring and All" (1923), in *The Collected Poems of William Carlos Williams*. Volume 1: 1909-1939. New York: New Directions Books.

Wittgenstein, L. (1968). *Philosophical Investigations*. Cambridge: Basil Blackwell.